THE LENNON TAPES

JOHN LENNON AND YOKO ONO
IN CONVERSATION WITH
ANDY PEEBLES 6 DECEMBER 1980

BRITISH BROADCASTING CORPORATION

Published by the
British Broadcasting Corporation
35 Marylebone High Street
London W1M 4AA

ISBN 0 563 17944 9

First published 1981
© BBC Publications 1981

Printed and bound in England by
Jolly & Barber Ltd, Rugby

FOREWORD

The original reason Andy Peebles and I planned to visit New York was to record an interview with David Bowie (broadcast on Radio One, 5 January 1981). Shortly before we set out I thought we should take the opportunity also to interview John Lennon and Yoko Ono. They had not spoken to anyone from radio for some years but with their new album just released I thought it possible they might agree to see us. With the help of WEA Records in Britain and Geffen Records in New York it was arranged that we could talk to John and Yoko on Saturday 6 December 1980 in the Hit Factory studio where they had recorded the new album.

If they had given us half an hour it would have been worthwhile, but in the event the interview lasted over three hours and we continued talking long after that over dinner! John was in good spirits, obviously enjoying life and keen to hear all the news from home.

We arrived back in London at breakfast time on Tuesday 9 December to be greeted with the awful news of John's murder. Many hours of Radio One output that day were devoted to his music, including a special hour at eleven-thirty in the morning in which Andy Peebles introduced some short excerpts from the interview which had suddenly taken on a new poignancy.

This book is transcribed from the whole interview which was first broadcast on Radio One with appropriate record inserts in five parts on Sundays, starting on 18 January 1981.

All royalties from the sale of the book will go to charities nominated by Yoko Ono and Andy Peebles.

PAUL WILLIAMS
Senior Producer, Radio One

INTRODUCTION

In the early hours of Sunday 7 December 1980 I shook hands and
said goodbye to John and Yoko Lennon. We were standing at
the entrance to Mr Chow's restaurant in New York. John
promised me he would be in touch when he came to London
early in 1981 and maybe he would come in and guest on my
morning show on Radio One. I told him he didn't need to call –
just to arrive any time he liked.

Our party of six had spent a marvellous couple of hours over
dinner. We had laughed and joked together, happy and
contented with our evening's work. To me it would become an
experience I would never forget.

The weekend in New York had included interviews with the
Lennons and David Bowie and a live broadcast direct to Britain
from New York. It had been, to say the least, a huge success.

When my producer Paul Williams had first discussed the
project I was both excited and apprehensive. We arrived on
Thursday 4 December and on the Friday met with Yoko to
discuss the next evening's interview. She confided in me that
John was just a little nervous about our encounter. Five years as
a near recluse had made him somewhat pensive at the prospect
of facing his first major radio interview. I told Yoko I was a little
nervous too and she seemed mildly amused.

The next evening at six p.m. I shook hands with John Lennon
in the Hit Factory studio where he and Yoko had recorded
Double Fantasy. From that moment onwards I knew things
would work out well – little did I know just how well. John
manifested himself as the finest interviewee it has ever been my
privilege to face. As you read the pages that follow I hope you

will derive some of the same feelings that I experienced during our three and a quarter hours in front of the microphone.

I will remember being confronted by a man full of conviction, honesty, humour and love – yes love – a love of life and a deep and tender love for his wife Yoko and son Sean.

Lennon leaves behind him some of the greatest music of my lifetime, music which will be treasured by our children and our children's children. The world of popular music in Great Britain mourns one of its greatest sons – and all he was saying was 'Give Peace a Chance'.

ANDY PEEBLES

THE INTERVIEW

ANDY PEEBLES: John and Yoko, it is more than wonderful to be able to talk to you after a very, very long time. We've been reminiscing, just before the tape started rolling . . .

JOHN LENNON: Right.

ANDY PEEBLES: And John, you've been talking about *Saturday Club*, so the memory is still working.

JOHN LENNON: Oh the memory is very, very good; it gets better when you get older actually; it gets more clear.

ANDY PEEBLES: You remember those glorious days.

JOHN LENNON: Bernie Andrews [a producer who worked with the Beatles in the early 1960s] and – I was just saying – I heard some of the tracks – somebody must have pirated them, Bernie – in America, you know. I've heard *Saturday Club*. We did a lot of tracks that were never recorded on record for *Saturday Club*. All the stuff we'd been doing at the Cavern or Hamburg and that. There was some good stuff and they were well recorded, too.

ANDY PEEBLES: But the interesting thing is that you . . .

JOHN LENNON: *Three Cool Cats*, I think we did.

ANDY PEEBLES: Did you? You've still got them in your collection?

JOHN LENNON: I think I picked up a pirate record of it, but I'm not sure, because I buy all the pirate records and file them away. I don't play them, you know. I keep them.

ANDY PEEBLES: So they're all in mint condition.

JOHN LENNON: Yeah. Stuff from Sweden and things like that, where there was good live shows done.

YOKO ONO: Do you think he has an American accent now?

7

ANDY PEEBLES: No, I don't. Anything but. In fact, I'm quite
surprised that the man sounds very Liverpudlian, if I may say
so.

JOHN LENNON: Well . . . I mean. What . . . what do you want?
What do you want? What do you want?

ANDY PEEBLES: Yoko, let me ask you. We're . . . John and I are
getting into reminiscing there. How much does all this mean to
you? How much . . . how much have you learnt through your
association with John about the days before you met?

YOKO ONO: Well, part of it's gibberish, and the other part is
fascinating, you know. I've learnt a lot, haven't I?

JOHN LENNON: Yeah, I've just about told her everything.

YOKO ONO: In a decade.

ANDY PEEBLES: A lot of history. We need to refresh people's
memories – I would like to refresh people's memories – as to
how you two actually met in the first place.

JOHN LENNON: Oh it's a long story. Yoko had come . . .

YOKO ONO: Met with a smash.

JOHN LENNON: Yeah . . . Yoko had come to London – or had
been invited to London – by some group of artists or
something called Destruction in Art Symposium, which was . . .
they had some big thing going on in London. And she had a . . .
an exhibition put on by that gallery – what was it called?
John . . .

YOKO ONO: Indica Gallery.

JOHN LENNON: Indica Gallery. Marianne Faithfull . . .

YOKO ONO: By John Dunbar.

JOHN LENNON: John Dunbar, Marianne Faithfull's ex-husband.
And he . . . I used to go down there occasionally; I'd been
down to see things like Takis who'd made these flashing lights
and sold them for a fortune. You know, it would be garbage.
But they sent me this pamphlet, or he called me – I don't know
which – about this Japanese girl from New York, who was
going to be in a bag, you know, doing this Event or Happening.
I thought – Hmm, you know, Sex. So I went down and it was
quite funny, because I had a chauffeur-driven SS Cooper-Mini
with black windows. You know, the chauffeur was about eight-
foot tall, and the Mini drives up, you know. A giant guy gets out

and opens the door, and I go in. And it's the night before the opening, and . . .

YOKO ONO: And I was in the basement.

JOHN LENNON: She was in the basement. I had no . . . there was nobody there, I was thinking . . .

ANDY PEEBLES: Just in the basement, not in the bag?

JOHN LENNON: No, she wasn't in the bag. So I go in . . .

YOKO ONO: I was preparing, you know, it was before the opening.

JOHN LENNON: There was, you know, like a few nails on a stand, and an apple on a stand – Cosmic – and just these strange looking objects. Just, you know, to look like Found Objects that had been painted white, with little messages written on them. So John Dunbar was showing me around and I was looking . . . what . . . how much is that? You know. A hundred pounds for a bag of nails? Are you kidding? How much is the apple? £200. I said . . .

YOKO ONO: Fresh apple.

JOHN LENNON: Oh fresh, thanks a lot. £200 for a fresh apple? I said . . . I thought this is . . . this is a con; what the hell is this, you know. I go downstairs and there's a few sort of . . . they must have been assistants, but I thought they were the . . . a minimal audience, lying around on the floor. Anyway, but Dunbar's trying to hustle a bit, because he thinks the Millionaire Beatle's coming to buy, you know. So he introduces me to this strange-looking Japanese woman. Nothing's happening in the bags. I'm expecting an orgy, you know. In a bag, you know. Something's going to be happening in a bag, you know, psychedelic. And it's all quiet. And he introduces me to her. And I said, Well where's the sort of happening, the event? She gives me a little card. And it just says 'Breathe' on it. So I said (*Breathes heavily*) – you mean like that? She says – yeah, that's it. So I'm looking for action, you know, and I see this thing called Hammer and Nail, and it's a board with a chain and a hammer hanging on it, and a bunch of nails at the bottom. I said – Well, can I hammer a nail in? She says no. So John Dunbar whisks her away . . .

YOKO ONO: This is before the opening, you know. I didn't want anybody to touch anything, you know.

ANDY PEEBLES: Right.

JOHN LENNON: So he takes her in a corner and says – That's a Millionaire, you know. You know who that is? She didn't know who I was, you know.

YOKO ONO: He didn't explain anything really. He was just sort of trying to . . . you know, hint, hint, you know, with his eyes.

JOHN LENNON: Well whatever, she came over and said, You can hammer one in for five shillings. I said – Are you . . . I'll give you an imaginary five shillings and hammer an imaginary nail in. All right? And that's when we fell. (*Sings*) Da, da, da, da, da.

ANDY PEEBLES: It was as easy as that, was it?

JOHN LENNON: Well, but it took a long time before we . . . I mean we were both very shy, you know. So the next time we met was a Claes Oldenburg opening with a lot of, you know, like soft . . . what was it? Objects like cheese-burgers made out of rubber and garbage like that. And we met again then and sort of made eye contact. But it was eighteen months to two years before we really got together.

ANDY PEEBLES: Do you remember what sort of frame of mind you were in in those days, John? Were you a happy man musically? Were you satisfied with life?

JOHN LENNON: What year? '66?

YOKO ONO: '66.

JOHN LENNON: Well you'd have to tell me what the Beatles . . .

YOKO ONO: End of . . .

JOHN LENNON: . . . had out then and I'll tell you what mood I was in, because I only remember things by what tracks were out.

ANDY PEEBLES: It's just that going on record you'd said at that time, after you'd done, I think I'm right in saying, the film *How I Won The War*, you said in the Press recently that at that stage you actually genuinely wanted out from the Beatles. The pressure was all too much.

JOHN LENNON: Well. It wasn't so much . . .

YOKO ONO: Oh, I didn't know that . . .

JOHN LENNON: . . . the pressure, it was the boredom, you

10

know. After the Beatles' last tour, which was '65, I think, with the one where the Klu Klux Klan were burning Beatle records and I was, you know, held up as a Satanist, or something. Then we decided, no more touring; that's enough of that. I'm not going to put up with it. And I was dead nervous, so I said 'Yes' to Dick Lester, that I would make this movie with him. I went to Almeria, Spain for six weeks, just to . . . because I didn't know what to do. What do you do when you don't tour? There's no life. Because I'd been on the road for . . .

ANDY PEEBLES: And that meant a lot to you, didn't it?

JOHN LENNON: Well, it wasn't that I wanted to tour so much, but I didn't know what to do. What . . . what the hell do you do all day, you know, I mean? (*Laughs*) So I went, I did the movie which was boring as hell and spent six weeks there. But I was really too scared to walk away. I was thinking, well, this is like the end really. You know, there's no more touring. That means there's going to be a blank space in the future. At some time or other that's when I really started considering what can one do? Considering the life without the Beatles – what would it be? And I spent that six weeks thinking about that. What would it . . . what would it . . . what am I going to do, you know? Am I going to be doing Vegas – I call it now . . . but cabaret? I mean, where do you go? So that's when I started thinking about it. But I could not think what . . . what it would be, or how I could do it, or . . . I didn't consider forming my own group or anything, because it didn't even enter my mind. Just what would I do when it stopped.

ANDY PEEBLES: But at some stage you obviously did consider that the two of you would make music together. Did that happen quickly?

JOHN LENNON: Well yes, as soon as we got into *Two Virgins*, I was interested.

ANDY PEEBLES: And this is going back to 1968, of course, the first time you . . .

YOKO ONO: But that just happened. *Two Virgins* just happened . . .

JOHN LENNON: Yes, *Two Virgins* happened by accident, yes. But still, once we'd . . . I realised somebody else was as kind of barmy as me, you know, a wife with sort of freaky sounds and could . . . could equally enjoy non-dance music or non-pop music that was . . . they call it avant-garde, but whatever it is, you know. Things to hear in an earphone.

ANDY PEEBLES: Did you feel it was avant-garde at the time? I mean we're going back now what . . . 1968 . . . twelve years. Did you see that as being . . . ?

JOHN LENNON: What? *Two Virgins*?

ANDY PEEBLES: . . . being very, very avant-garde?

JOHN LENNON: Well that's the only word you can use for it. But, you know, I think a label like avant-garde defeats itself, you know. You learnt to have avant-garde exhibitions. The very fact that avant-garde can have an exhibition defeats the purpose of avant-garde, because it's already formalised and ritualised, so it's not avant-garde. But that was the only word . . . that was the word that was applied to her and her ilk.

YOKO ONO: Sort of loosely.

JOHN LENNON: But I didn't think anything of it other than, you know, variations on a theme of sound.

ANDY PEEBLES: 1969, in April, the Beatles of course had a smash hit back home in the UK with *Get Back*. What was your sort of frame of mind as far as the Beatles still having hits was concerned, when you'd already started on what was to be a very different musical relationship? Did it matter to you?

JOHN LENNON: I wasn't consciously making any decisions. It was all sort of subconscious and I just made the records with the Beatles like one goes to one's job at nine in the morning, you know. I mean, Paul or whoever would say, 'It's time to make a record'. I'd just go in and make a record, you know, and not think too much about it. Always I've enjoyed the session if it was a good session. You know, if we got our rocks off, playing, it was fine. If it was a drag, it was a drag. But it was . . . it had become a job.

ANDY PEEBLES: Now in 1969, also in April, you did *Rape*, which was a TV Documentary in Vienna. How . . .

JOHN LENNON: Well it was filmed in London, for Austrian TV.

ANDY PEEBLES: Right, for Austrian TV. How did that come about?

JOHN LENNON: Well, do you want me to answer, or she can . . . ?

ANDY PEEBLES: Yoko, . . .

JOHN LENNON: It's your film.

YOKO ONO: Well it was just a filmic idea about just following a girl, and keep following and just filming her, and what would happen to somebody who's totally exposed all the time, you know. And well in a way, I mean, I didn't think about it then, but . . . because that filmic idea was something that I thought before I really got together with John, so . . . But it was very interesting that in a way the Beatles were in that position, and John obviously was in a position of constantly being followed by camera, you know. But we did it with this girl, this sort of . . . We picked a girl – well, we didn't pick this girl, the cameraman picked a girl, and he just kept on following the girl, and the girl kept saying, Well why are you doing this? Why are you doing this, you know. And finally, somehow they made an arrangement so that they got a key for the girl's apartment . . .

JOHN LENNON: From her sister.

YOKO ONO: Oh is that . . . ? So – and she didn't know about this, and she went into her apartment of course. These guys are still filming her, you know. So she freaked out and it's just a beautiful scene where she's saying, Why is this? Why is this happening to me? And she was hiding her face and everything, you know.

JOHN LENNON: She was a tourist in London and she was picked out of the blue. We used to send the cameraman out every day for test shooting in the park, in Hyde Park, and he'd pick somebody, and we'd look at the rushes of different people he'd started following round. And then finally we selected this girl and said, Okay go back, you know, because he knew which house she'd come out of. And I . . . she was Austrian, or something . . .

YOKO ONO: Beautiful girl.

JOHN LENNON: Beautiful girl. Claimed to be an actress after the film came out.

ANDY PEEBLES: I'm sure she did . . . (Laughter)

JOHN LENNON: Right. But . . . and also, we were accused of

setting it up, that she knew all about it. But she didn't at all know about it.

ANDY PEEBLES: A new-found career for somebody who'd never dreamt it would happen to her.

JOHN LENNON: But talking of bags, what we did was, we went to the famous hotel in Vienna, to put it on the TV there. It caused a riot; it was the biggest reaction Austrian TV had ever had. I mean there was complaints; there was no sex in it; it was just a constant . . . you think something's going to happen all the time, but nothing ever really happens. Just the pressure on the girl as she's cracking up under the strain of these strange people following her around. And . . . but the Austrians never saw us . . . What's the hotel? The Chocolate Cake Hotel – it used to be the Hapsburg's Castle or whatever. And we were in there, but we . . . they never saw us, the Austrian Press. We did everything in a bag. So we came down to the Press Conference in a bag, in the elevator. And the front page of the Austrian papers was all these people holding mikes to a bag, you know. And all they said was, But John, is that really you? I'd say Yeah, it's me. But how do we know? I said, Because I'm telling you. They said, Well, will you sing a song? You know. I sang *Maggie May* and she sang some Japanese . . .

YOKO ONO: . . . some Japanese songs.

JOHN LENNON: . . . folk songs to them in the bag. And a guy said, I've . . . but I've waited years to see you. Why did you have to pick Austria to go in a bag? I said, Because we wanted to.

ANDY PEEBLES: You did want to but, looking back on it now, how do you feel about that sort of thing now, because it got amazing reaction, didn't it, from some people . . .

YOKO ONO: Oh, but it was great, you know.

ANDY PEEBLES: You're smiling and giggling about it now . . .

JOHN LENNON: We love it.

ANDY PEEBLES: Do you think you'd have smiled and giggled about it then?

JOHN LENNON: We were . . . Are you kidding? You ought to have seen what we were doing in the bag. We were cracking up in there. (*Snorts*) Like that. On some of the bag events; one

14

of them was . . . our Rolls-Royce . . . We didn't go to some Royal Command opening of a movie or something. We sent two Hare Krishna kids in the back, and it was in all the English papers – John and Yoko arriving. But the . . . for some reason or other, the chauffeur . . .

YOKO ONO: By mistake.

JOHN LENNON: . . . by mistake, arrived after Princess Margaret. So the thing in the English papers was 'How Dare They Insult the Queen', or Princess Margaret, by having their car arrive late. Well, we didn't plan that at all, and we said Well, if anybody asks you any questions, just keep singing Hare Krishna to them; they'll think it's John and Yoko anyway. They're that daft enough to sing Hare Krishna. It must be John and Yoko. We watched it on TV, you know, peeing in our pants. (*Laughter*)

ANDY PEEBLES: Let's move to June, 1969, and the *Ballad of John and Yoko* went to Number One in Britain, and was Top Ten in this country. Did that give you a feeling of satisfaction and of achievement, as a duo, that you'd got a great success with what has since become . . . ?

YOKO ONO: We never thought of it like that.

JOHN LENNON: I never thought about it. No, I didn't even remember it was Number One. No, it was just we were in Paris.

YOKO ONO: We were so busy doing things.

JOHN LENNON: We were . . . you know, I mean that period we were doing films, records, together, with the Beatles, bed-ins, and it was just quite crazy.

ANDY PEEBLES: But did you want to . . . did you want to detach yourselves as two people? I mean you mentioned that you were still . . .

JOHN LENNON: No, because the *Ballad of John and Yoko* was . . . Paul and I made that record. He was . . . he played bass and drums and I played guitar and sang, you know.

ANDY PEEBLES: And in the back of your mind, was there a feeling that John and Yoko by this time definitely wanted to go their own way and create their own music?

YOKO ONO: No, we didn't think of it like that. Nothing definite

15

like that. We were just so busy and involved with things that we were doing. And we got so inspired every minute you know, and so maybe it just sort of took a natural course and . . .

JOHN LENNON: Yeah. You know, she would just sort of be around, and we'd make . . . had the Beatles been less tense about her, there probably would have been some. There was a couple of jam sessions in *Let It Be*, with Yoko and the Beatles playing, but they never got in the movie of course. But I understand it all now, but then we thought well, you know, why isn't . . . She just wanted to join in everything.

YOKO ONO: (*over*) It was a fantastic jam, you know.

JOHN LENNON: You know, just join in whatever was going on. So we had no conscious thing about, Well, we're here and they're there. We were just making music.

ANDY PEEBLES: You said they were tense, John. Was that because they feared an intervention, or because they feared that the two of you would eventually go your own ways and that would be it?

JOHN LENNON: Well look . . . I don't know whether they were conscious. I think, looking back you know, I understand there'd be four guys very close together and the women had . . . that we were with them, wives or girlfriends, had been, you know, the old-fashioned type of female that we all know and love, you know; the one that was in . . .

YOKO ONO: . . . know and love.

JOHN LENNON: . . . in the kitchen all the time, with the baby, and you never, you know, she never came to the sessions even. You never saw the wives, only for openings and . . . when they did their hair, you know. And suddenly we were together all the time, you know. Sort of in a corner mumbling and giggling together and doing *Two Virgins* and bags, and there were Paul, George and Ringo saying, What the hell are they doing? What's happened to him? You know. And my attention completely went off them. Now it wasn't deliberate. It was just like I was so involved and intrigued with what we were doing, that I . . . and then we'd look round and see that we weren't being approved. But I understand how they felt, because if it had been Paul or George or Ringo that had fallen

16

in love with somebody and got totally involved suddenly, it wasn't like, you know, somebody . . . George coming and saying, I'm going to work with Eric Clapton and the Band now, and screw you. It wasn't that kind of thing at all. It was just suddenly this involvement.

YOKO ONO: You know, it wasn't in our consciousness at all. And I was just amazed because, you know, I didn't know anything about England really, you know. I was always in New York, so to speak. And to me he was another Englishman. I didn't know about the Liverpool and that, you know, that sort of thing.

JOHN LENNON: Just another Englishman, my dear.

YOKO ONO: Well, you know what I'm talking about. And just sort of . . . he looked sort of . . . the first impression I got from him was – He's sort of handsome and, you know, sort of nice, and tender, I thought. Anyway, so I didn't know about all this macho trip, you know, that they were on. You know. It was a real surprise.

ANDY PEEBLES: An interesting . . . interesting way of putting it. It really is. A macho trip.

YOKO ONO: Well. Yes, I know what you mean. I mean Beatle music is now a macho trip, you know. And that's true. And he did look very nice and sort of . . . The feminine side of the society was represented by them in a way. You know, there was that too. So, I didn't realise that. I mean he . . . they didn't come on at the box or anything, you know.

ANDY PEEBLES: We'll talk more about the feminine side of society I think, a little bit later on. If we move to May 1969 . . .

JOHN LENNON: You mean Benny Hill.

ANDY PEEBLES: (*Laughter*) You have got a good memory. He's on over here, isn't he?

JOHN LENNON: No, he's on over here all the time. Tommy Cooper. There's so many English programmes on, in New York especially, that you see everything.

ANDY PEEBLES: Now you've brought the subject up, and before we go any further and move to the Unfinished Music Number Two, let me just ask you . . .

JOHN LENNON: 'Life with the Lyons', right, Bebe Daniels and Ben . . .

17

ANDY PEEBLES: Ah . . . now we're back with the BBC programmes again, aren't we? It still obviously means a lot to you. You've got a memory for all the names. As you sit here in New York on this day, watching English television programmes, do you ever get the itch to think, Ah, it would be nice to go back and have a look?

JOHN LENNON: Oh yeah, but you know, but as I always say to any Englishman I meet . . . most English people I meet are ex-pat . . . expatriates, you know. I mean, as I was saying offstage before, I've been to Singapore, Hong Kong, Cape Town, Johannesburg, and all points East, and the Caribbean, and the Pacific places where, you know, Noël Coward and Somerset Maugham and all those people that I like to read and read about were. And the famous place in Singapore, the Hotel Rattles or Ruffles or something where they'd all be.

ANDY PEEBLES: Raffles, yes.

JOHN LENNON: So, as Churchill said, it's the Englishman's inaliable [*sic*] right to live where the hell he likes. And so . . . and as I say to any Englishman who says, Well don't you get homesick and come back? I say, What do you think, it's going to vanish? It's not going to be there when I . . . when I want to go back?

YOKO ONO: But he's very English at heart you know. And I mean just this morning he was just looking at this book and suddenly . . . it was just this coincidence because, you know, we're meeting you now, you know, and this all very English scene. But, and he saw this Liverpool in this book and he started choking up, you know, really. Oh, Liverpool. (*Laughter*)

JOHN LENNON: I'm supposed to be tough, you know.

YOKO ONO: Yeah, I know what you mean. But the combination's very peculiar, you know. The macho side and the . . . the other side.

JOHN LENNON: It's a traditional English thing, from Drake or whatever on, to go everywhere, you know. But I do find myself in English parts of the world, and it's very interesting.

ANDY PEEBLES: Do you have many English friends in New York at the moment, John?

JOHN LENNON: Well, as the *Moonlight on the Water* song

18

says, 'No friends and yet no enemies'. I'm either working, or family-orientated. I don't do a lot of . . .

YOKO ONO: Socialising.

JOHN LENNON: Socialising with . . . with people of any nationality. And offhand I can't think of anybody, English or American, I particularly hang around with. We're . . . we've been self-involved since we met and we're complete . . . totally self-contained.

YOKO ONO: Self-contained.

JOHN LENNON: I mean when Elton or Bowie or Mick are around and we're in the mood to . . . to mix, we see them. They're English, right. I forget, you see. I don't . . . I don't always divide people into nationality, you know. I mean it's just Bowie's in town, I'll do an *Elephant Man*.

ANDY PEEBLES: Yeah, we saw it last night.

JOHN LENNON: I haven't seen it, but, you know, I would consider him a friend and/or acquaintance . . . I don't know how close you'd put it. Because I worked with him, and we both know him and so that in that respect, whoever . . . The Rockers that come through, I see them.

ANDY PEEBLES: So if we go back to May, '69, and we talk about *Life With The Lions*. Yoko, you were in bed on the cover, I think I'm right in saying?

YOKO ONO: Yes. We had a miscarriage or something didn't we?

JOHN LENNON: You had a miscarriage and I was there, the actual reality of it.

YOKO ONO: That's right, exactly.

ANDY PEEBLES: Because you'd had great problems, hadn't you, conceiving?

YOKO ONO: I know. We had many miscarriages.

JOHN LENNON: We did.

YOKO ONO: Yes, about three.

JOHN LENNON: Yeah, enough to make us miserable about it, you know. Think we could never have a child. But we did. It turned out to . . . one . . . an English doctor told me, something wrong with my sperm, you know, because of the hard life I'd led. And he said I could never have a baby, that we could never have a baby, because of me. But we met this Chinese acupuncturist in San Francisco. He said, What about your wife? You have baby. Just be good boy. Eat well. No drugs. No drink. So that's what I did. And we had a baby.

ANDY PEEBLES: And Sean is living proof.

JOHN LENNON: He is, yes.

ANDY PEEBLES: He is, right.

YOKO ONO: Oh he's fantastic, yes.

ANDY PEEBLES: Briefly dealing with that album, one side was called *Cambridge '69*. That interests me. Why *Cambridge '69*?

YOKO ONO: Well that was funny because that was around the time that . . . why was it '69, though, that . . . well, anyway.

JOHN LENNON: I know the story backwards, but you can tell it.

YOKO ONO: I was invited . . . Oh, go ahead, you can . . .

JOHN LENNON: No, it was your story.

YOKO ONO: I was invited to Cambridge to do a number, you know, a sort of avant-garde number.

JOHN LENNON: This was independent of me, though. It was nothing to do with me.

YOKO ONO: And they didn't realise that we were together, so to speak.

ANDY PEEBLES: This was to do with the University . . .

JOHN LENNON: Yes, Cambridge University.

YOKO ONO: This was just before we got married I suppose. So, they didn't realise then and they invited me, and so I said, Well, all right, what shall I do? And John was saying, Well, it's all right, why don't you go? And they were saying, Well, are you going to bring a band, or what, you know? So John said, Well, I'm the band, but don't tell them, you know. I'll be the band, you know. So I say, Yes, I'll bring a band, you know, band with me.

JOHN LENNON: And we arrived in Cambridge, it was supposed to be a avant-garde – that word again – jazz thing, right. And there was a guy called John Tchicai who was apparently a famous avant-garde sax guy, or jazz sax guy – I didn't know any of them. A few people that I don't remember the names of. They were there too. And I turned up as her band, you know. And the people were looking and saying, Is it? Is it? you know. I just had a guitar and an amp and that was the first time I'd played that style, just pure feedback and whatever it is on that track. And the audience were very weird, because they were all these sort of intellectual artsey-fartsies from Cambridge, you know, and they were uptight because the rock and roll guy was there, even though I wasn't doing any rhythm. If you hear it, it's just pure sound. Because what else can you do when a woman's howling, you know, you just go along with it, right?

YOKO ONO: They were totally solid, you know, very polite.

JOHN LENNON: They were totally solid. Well, the reaction I got from the quotes, unquotes, avant-garde group – not only in Cambridge, it was the same reaction that she got from the rock and roll people, like, What's she doing here? – well, when I was doing the stuff with her, this little tight-knit avant-garde scene would be saying, What the hell . . . who the hell is he? He's one of those pop . . . So we're both getting schtick for not being in the right bag.

YOKO ONO: Do you think they noticed . . . do you think they noticed, because I mean . . .

JOHN LENNON: You bet they noticed. They were trying so hard not to notice. You know that when you go in a restaurant. You can always tell people are trying not to look at you. You know, they're being cool, and you pick up this sort of vibes, or whatever you call it, coming from people not looking at you, you know. It's worse than when they look.

ANDY PEEBLES: So that was Cambridge, 1969.

JOHN LENNON: That's Cambridge, 1969.

ANDY PEEBLES: A visit to the University.

JOHN LENNON: Right, right.

ANDY PEEBLES: Back in '69, July the fourth, the Plastic Ono Band single *Give Peace a Chance*. Which was Number Two in Britain. And I think it's still regarded by a great number of people as being a bit of a classic.

JOHN LENNON: Great.

ANDY PEEBLES: Refresh our memories as to why you put that particular song together, because you've fought for a lot of causes, haven't you, the both of you over the years?

JOHN LENNON: Yeah, well, after . . . We first did the Bed-In in Amsterdam, and the initial reaction to the Bed-In was very . . . The point of the Bed-In in a nutshell was a commercial for Peace, as opposed to a commercial for War, which was on the news every day those days in the newspapers. Every day it was dismembered bodies and napalm and we thought, Well, why don't they have something nice in the newspapers. That old thing, you know. And anyway, we did the Bed-In. What the Bed-In was was seven days – because the Press were always asking questions, asking questions. Seven days that they can ask anything – no secrets, you know, no time limit. Like, you know, you come in and take the photographs and then the photographers go away and then the Press are allowed ten minutes to ask . . . This was you come in as long as you like, till you've got everything you need to know about John and Yoko, or what we stand for or what we are.

ANDY PEEBLES: Which, knowing the Press as I vaguely do, must have dumbfounded them actually, as an offer.

JOHN LENNON: Well, I tell you the big . . . one of the most hysterical moments was the first day when Don Short and all the gang, and Donald Zec and all them, they were fighting like crazy . . . we were sitting in there, you know, Amsterdam Hilton, in the bed like two little kids, you know, with all the posters on the wall . . .

YOKO ONO: Flower children.

JOHN LENNON: Flower kids, or whatever. These guys were sweating to fight to get in first because they thought we were going to be doing . . . making love in bed, you see; that's where their minds were at.

YOKO ONO: How could they think that?

JOHN LENNON: Because we'd been naked . . . naked, bed, John and Yoko, sex. So anyway, try and cut this story down, because they all of them go on for ever, there's so many links to it. We did it again. We tried to do it in New York, but the American government wouldn't let us in. They knew we'd done it in Amsterdam; they didn't want any peaceniks here, which is what we heard the Department of whoever controls that said. Well, we ended up doing it in Montreal instead, and broadcast it across the border, you see. And there was live riots at Berkeley at the Bed-In in Amsterdam. But after answering all these questions, many, many, many, many, many, many, many, many times, it got down to all we were saying was, Give Peace a Chance. Not we have any formula or Communism or Socialism will answer it or any '-ism' could answer it. We didn't have a format or a . . . we couldn't give you a plan . . .

ANDY PEEBLES: . . . but just sit there and . . .

JOHN LENNON: . . . but just consider the idea of . . . of not having this war, just consider it. So that's what, we, in a nutshell, we were saying. So we recorded it in the bedroom of a Montreal Hilton or whatever hotel we were in.

ANDY PEEBLES: On an eight-track machine which you had brought up to the room, I gather.

JOHN LENNON: Up to the room, yeah. And there was like Tommy Smothers and Tim Leary and Dick Gregg, and all people sort of clapping along and singing on the chorus. And if you hear the record, it's funny actually, because my rhythm sense has always been a bit wild, and halfway through it, I got on the on-beat instead of the back-beat and it was hard because all the . . . there was non-musicians playing along with us. And so I had to put a lot of tape echo to double up the beat to keep a steady beat right through the whole record, so it goes Bo-boom, Bo-boom, instead of Ba, Ba.

YOKO ONO: It's the thought that counts.

ANDY PEEBLES: It was the thought.

JOHN LENNON: And I sort of cheated. The word Masturbation was in it but I wrote in the lyric sheet, because I'd had enough of the bannings of all . . . every bloody record I put out was banned for some reason or another. Even *Walrus* was banned on the BBC at one time, because it said 'Knickers'. So I mean I'd been banned so many times all over, that I copped out and wrote 'Mastication'.

YOKO ONO: Anyway, it's not a cop-out. It was a consideration because it's the song that has to go round the world, you know. And unless . . .

JOHN LENNON: Yeah. It was more important to get it out than be bothered by a word, Masturbation.

ANDY PEEBLES: And probably the first time and the last time that the hotel in Montreal had been asked for an eight-track recording machine on Room Service.

JOHN LENNON: Yeah. That's right. (*Laughs*)

ANDY PEEBLES: *Peace in Toronto*, the live album where you teamed up with Eric Clapton and Klaus Voorman and Alan White. Now Klaus, I remember, was with Manfred Mann's band, so he was an old mate. What about . . .?

JOHN LENNON: And he was from Hamburg.

ANDY PEEBLES: That's right, from the days that . . .

JOHN LENNON: We met him in Hamburg. He was an illustrator for record covers in Germany.

ANDY PEEBLES: This goes back to sort of Barry Fantoni era doesn't it?

JOHN LENNON: 1961 . . .

ANDY PEEBLES: Right.

JOHN LENNON: . . . when we met Klaus Voorman, 1962 maybe.

ANDY PEEBLES: And Eric? What was the tie-up with Eric? Because I remember Eric with the Yardbirds, and . . .

JOHN LENNON: Well, Eric had been a friend of George's. You know, the guitarists all tend to hang out together . . .

ANDY PEEBLES: Yes, the lead men.

JOHN LENNON: Yeah. And we were in that exuberant period, and we got this phone call from Toronto on a Friday night, because there was a Rock 'n' Roll Revival show in Toronto, with a hundred thousand audience or whatever it was; and that Chuck was going to be there and Jerry Lee was going to be there. And all the great rockers who were still living, and Bo Diddley and, supposedly the Doors were top of the bill.

YOKO ONO: The Friday night thing I'm not sure about. Remember, Bruce . . . they came to Bruce to discuss it and all that . . . whatever . . .

JOHN LENNON: Ah well, whatever . . . it was very, very quick. We didn't have a band then. W didn't even have a group that had played with us for more than half a minute.

ANDY PEEBLES: I bet you didn't have too much trouble getting people to come and . . .

JOHN LENNON: Called Eric. It was . . . I couldn't find him; I don't know where the hell he was. I finally got through to him. I got Klaus, and we got Alan White, because we'd cut *Instant Karma* around that period, so I'd met him; he'd been on that. And I said, Look, there's this thing on in Toronto, do you want to come? They said, Okay. Now we didn't know what to play, because we'd never played together before, the band. And on the airplane we're running through these oldies, so the rehearsal for that record, which turned into not a bad record, was on the plane with electric guitars, so you . . . not even acoustic, you couldn't hear . . . saying – Are we doing the Elvis version of *Blue Suede Shoes* . . . or the Carl Perkins, you know, with the different break at the beginning, Ta-jing-jing instead of De . . . whatever. And that's what we were doing, we just wrote this list . . . I hadn't got the words to any of the songs. I knew *Dizzy Miss Lizzie*, but there was a couple . . . but *Blue Suede Shoes* and a couple I hadn't done since Liverpool, in the Cavern. And that's all we could do. And we went on, and we were so nervous because we didn't know what we were doing, and she was going to do her pieces, *Don't Worry Kyoko*, you know, which lasted thirty minutes. And we went on. It was fantastic. It was just getting dark. The lights were just going down. This was the first time I ever heard about this – I'd never seen it anywhere else; I think it was the first time it happened – they all lit candles, or lights, and the sun was just going down, there was fifty or sixty thousand, I don't . . .

YOKO ONO: It was gorgeous.

ANDY PEEBLES: I remember the reports, yes.

JOHN LENNON: And all these candles lit up and it was really beautiful, you know. And we sort of . . . the vibes were fantastic, and we did the string of rock 'n' roll stuff. Then we finished with Yoko's number, because you can't go anywhere after you've reached that sort of pitch. And, to end the show, I just said, Look, at the end, when she's finished doing whatever she's doing, just put . . . lean your guitars on the amps and let it keep howling. And we can get off like that. Because you can't very well go Ji-jing like the Beatles and bow at the end of screaming and fifty watts of feedback.

ANDY PEEBLES: Exit on feedback.

JOHN LENNON: And we tried to put it out on Capitol, and Capitol didn't want to put it out. They said, This is garbage; we're not going to put it out with her screaming on one side and you doing this sort of live stuff. And they just refused to put it out. But we finally persuaded them that, you know, people might buy this. Of course it went gold the next day. And then, the funny thing was – this is a side story – Klein had got a deal on that record that it was a John and Yoko Plastic Ono record, not a Beatles record, so we could get a higher royalty, because the Beatles' royalties were so low; they'd been locked in in '63 – and Capitol said, Sure you can have it, you know. Nobody's going to buy that crap. They just threw it away and gave it us. And it came out, and it was fairly successful and it went gold. I don't know what chart position, but I've got a gold record somewhere that says . . . And four years later, we go to collect the royalties, and you know what they say? This is a Beatle record. So Capitol have it in my file under Beatle records. Isn't it incredible?

ANDY PEEBLES: It is. And you included on it *Yer Blues* from the White Album.

JOHN LENNON: *Yer Blues*, yeah. Because I'd done . . . I think I'd worked *Yer Blues* with Eric on the Rock 'n' Roll circus show of Mick, the Rolling Stones Show. They . . . John and Yoko appeared on that show, too.

YOKO ONO: A film of it.

JOHN LENNON: There was a film of it, but of course Mick never put it out, because . . . whatever. And there was me, Eric Clapton, Keith Richard on bass. I can't remember the drummer. And I did *Yer Blues* and then Yoko came on and did her Blues, you know. And there was some crazy violinist. So I . . . Eric knew that number, so two of us knew that number. We all knew *Blue Suede Shoes*. And so we just sort of picked the numbers like that. Offhand I don't recall what other songs are on it.

ANDY PEEBLES: You're smiling while you're telling me. It sounds as though in those days you were enjoying the freedom to be able to do something like that, which was instantly creative.

JOHN LENNON: Oh . . . it was instantly creative, and there was no big palaver, you know. It wasn't like this set format show that I'd been doing with the Beatles, where you'd go on and do these same numbers *I Wanna Hold Your Head* [sic], you know. And . . . the show lasts twenty minutes, you know, and nobody's listening, they're just screaming, and the amps are as big as a peanut. And, you know, it was more of a spectacular rather than rock 'n' roll. Whereas actually the first time I performed without the Beatles for years was the Rock and Roll Circus, and it was great to be on stage with Eric and Keith Richard and a different noise coming out behind me, even though I was still singing and playing the same style. It was just a great experience. I thought, Wow, it's fun with other people, you know.

ANDY PEEBLES: Romping through a career with John and Yoko. November 1969, the *Wedding Album.* What are your thoughts on that? Oh yes, with a wedding certificate, and a . . . you get a piece of cake included in the box?

JOHN LENNON: No, a photograph of John, a photograph of a piece of cake. It was like our sharing our wedding with whoever wanted to share it with us. We didn't expect a hit record out of it. It was more of a . . . that's why we called it *Wedding Album.* You know, people make a wedding album, show it to the relatives when they come round. Well, our relatives are the . . . what you call fans, or people that follow us outside. So that was our way of letting them join in on the wedding. And I think you sang *No Bed for Beatle John* then?

YOKO ONO: Yes, I think so.

JOHN LENNON: Or was that on *Life With The Lions*?

YOKO ONO: I don't remember.

JOHN LENNON: (*Sings*) 'No bed for Beatle John . . .' she was singing newspaper clippings.

ANDY PEEBLES: November, '69. .

JOHN LENNON: I mean a part of Amsterdam, sorry, Bed-In, some of the interviews and talks that went on . . .

YOKO ONO: It was Peace and Love, symbolic of, you know, Wedding and . . .

JOHN LENNON: And we got married in Gibraltar, the Rock.

ANDY PEEBLES: That's right. The Rock.

JOHN LENNON: The British Rock.

ANDY PEEBLES: Any particular reason for getting married in Gibraltar?

JOHN LENNON: We couldn't . . . we wanted to get married on a cross-channel ferry. That was the romantic part, when we went to Southampton and then we couldn't get on because she wasn't English and she couldn't get that Day Visa to go across and they said, Anyway, you can't get married. The Captain's not allowed to do it any more. So we were in Paris and we were calling Peter Brown, who was working . . . who's now with Robert Stigwood, RSO, so we called him and said, We want to get married. Where can we go? And he called back and said, Gibraltar's the only place. So – Okay, let's go. And we went there and it was beautiful. It's the Pillar of Hercules, and also symbolically they called it the End of the World at one period. There's some name besides Pillar of Hercules. But they thought the world outside was the . . . a mystery from there, so that was like the Gateway to the World. So we liked it in the symbolic sense, and the Rock foundation of our relationship.

ANDY PEEBLES: November '69, *Cold Turkey*, which was . . .

YOKO ONO: (*Shrill squeal*)

ANDY PEEBLES: . . . Top Twenty in the UK. And got to Number Thirty in America, I think.

JOHN LENNON: Yeah. It was banned here as well. They thought it was a pro-drugs song, you know. It was just the . . .

ANDY PEEBLES: What was it to you, John? Was it something that was very important?

JOHN LENNON: Yeah, because, as always, I've always expressed what I've been feeling or thinking at the time, however badly or not, you know, from being . . . from early Beatle records on. It got . . . became more conscious later. But . . . so I was just show . . . writing the experience I'd had of withdrawing from heroin and saying, you know, this is what I thought when I was withdrawing, you know . . .

YOKO ONO: But also musically it was very interesting. I mean, it did . . .

JOHN LENNON: Yeah, Eric Clapton was on that too.

YOKO ONO: Yes. And also, we did attempt a few musically advanced interesting things, and . . .

JOHN LENNON: Yeah, Marc Bolan said it was the only new thing that had happened since the original Beatles, when it came out. But I wasn't thinking I'm going to make a new sound. But it was pretty what they call minimal now. Just bass drums and guitar.

ANDY PEEBLES: But it was banned in America.

JOHN LENNON: It was banned because it referred to drugs, and instead of using it as an example of, you know, Look, this guy is saying this is . . . It was like, to me, it was a Rock 'n' Roll version of *The Man with the Golden Arm.* You know, it's like banning *The Man with the Golden Arm*, because it showed Frank Sinatra suffering from drug . . . drug withdrawal. To ban the record is the same thing. It's like banning the movie. Because it shows reality.

ANDY PEEBLES: Does it amuse you that people's attitudes have changed over the years? Perhaps 'amused' is totally the wrong word. What are your feelings? I mean, drugs were something that we all lived with, I think, in our business, back in the Sixties. In the Seventies, the subject seemed to go underground because it was accepted by society, which to me is always a strange irony. Because people suddenly say, Well, okay, maybe it isn't so bad. How do you both look at it now, as people that were involved in it, for want of a better phrase, and were, in your case, were honest enough to come out and put something down musically on the subject?

JOHN LENNON: I don't . . . I don't think about it that much . . .

YOKO ONO: It's just like it's a trip that we went through. But at the same time now, it's clean up time and we're really sort of like cleaning our bodies and, you know, it's very important that.

JOHN LENNON: I don't think . . . it's just strange when you hear people are snorting in the White House and that stuff, you know, after the misery they put a lot of people through, and the night they bust us in England. And . . . we were planted. And I have now a stain on my . . . I have a record for life because the cop who bust me and Yoko, and also bust Brian Jones and the

Stones – he was scalp-hunting and making a name for himself. And I have a record for life. I have problems getting in countries because this guy bust me. I've never denied having been involved in drugs. There was a question raised in the Houses of Parliament, why do they need forty cops to arrest John and Yoko? I mean that thing was set up. The *Daily Mail* and the *Daily Express* were there, before the cops came. He'd called the Press. In fact, Don Short had told us 'they're coming to get you' three weeks before. So, believe me, I'd cleaned the house out, because Jimi Hendrix had lived there before in this apartment, and I'm not stupid. I went through the whole damn house.

ANDY PEEBLES: And it caused you a lot of heartache, I know that . . .

JOHN LENNON: It caused me a lot of heartache, and it still does. So I don't want . . . I wanted to know on how do I get rid of a record? Because the Statute of Appeals ran out, because I don't have a legal mind and I went to find out about it at one time, because I wanted to get this thing off my record. And they told me – Oh you should have applied within the first two years. But nobody told me that, and the only reason I pleaded guilty was because I thought they'd send Yoko away because we weren't married. And I thought – what's the word? – they'd throw her out of the country. So I copped the plea. And the cop said to me – Well, we've got you now, so it's nothing personal, you know, so . . . I've got a record; and I have problems all round the world because of that record.

YOKO ONO: Was that arrest after *Cold Turkey*?

JOHN LENNON: Probably.

ANDY PEEBLES: I think it probably was. I think it probably was.

YOKO ONO: Because you see I was just thinking . . .

JOHN LENNON: Well *Life With The Lions*, the back . . . the picture on the back of *Life With The Lions, Unfinished Music Number Two*, is us being dragged out of the Police Station; it's from newspaper pictures.

YOKO ONO: And yet they say that a blind man has an honest face because he doesn't know how to control the muscles and express himself with . . . using the muscles on their faces, you know. Sort of try to make a fictitious expression or something. They can't do that because they . . . they don't see their face. And it's almost like that. An artist, as you know, if you get truly inspired and something comes through you, like songs or poetry or whatever, then it's part of your experience you know, so the thing is you can't lie, you know, in your work somehow. It's . . . you can't lie, you know. And so, we were just sort of always bringing out songs that reflect our life, and like *Cold Turkey* you know was something that reflected our life, you know. And that's the kind of thing that always brings you trouble doesn't it. I mean . . .

ANDY PEEBLES: Honesty is not always the best policy.

JOHN LENNON: Seems like it. But still, you know, I prefer it. Because it's harder to live with the phony than it is with the real sort of causes, harassments in a physical sense or an outside sense. I found that the other way causes internal problems. You've been conning yourself or fooling yourself, which is quite easy for all of us. We're all so good at it, you know. That you don't even realise you're doing it. But in a way you pay a different kind of price for that. It's like the Oscar Wilde thing, you know, with the face growing old upstairs on the portrait, that one. It's that one.

YOKO ONO: So from around *Cold Turkey* we started to really pay our dues in a way, you know, for being honest.

JOHN LENNON: Yes, it was about seven and six, wasn't it. Three p they call it now, you know. You know, I don't even know how to count English money.

ANDY PEEBLES: Really?

JOHN LENNON: And I hardly know what American money is in change. I know that one is a twenty-five cent. I haven't learnt all those little nickels and those ones, so . . . if I went back to England, I wouldn't know what . . . how to buy anthing, or pay for anything. I've no idea what they're talking about. It was 12/6 when I left.

ANDY PEEBLES: Oh . . . yes, I could talk to you for hours about Decimalisation, but I better hadn't. I think we were all pretty well conned there.

JOHN LENNON: Yeah, you were. Right.

ANDY PEEBLES: Just before Christmas, 1969, you did a concert at the Lyceum in the Strand in London, with the Plastic Ono Band, including George Harrison, Billy Preston – one of my favourites – and the late, lamented Keith Moon, God Bless him – what a wonderful character.

JOHN LENNON: Yeah, and Bonnie and Delaney's [sic] whole band.

ANDY PEEBLES: That's right.

JOHN LENNON: We were talking about that yesterday, funnily enough.

YOKO ONO: Mmm. Oh yes, that's right.

JOHN LENNON: It was a Unicef concert.

YOKO ONO: It's amazing that it's recorded. I mean, I can remember it.

JOHN LENNON: Oh great, there's somebody who remembers it. Because . . . we were doing the show, and George and Bonnie and Delaney and all those . . . Billy and all that crowd turned up. They'd just come back from Sweden, and George had been playing Invisible Man in Bonnie and Delaney's Band, which Eric Clapton had been doing, to get the pressure off being the famous Eric and the famous George. They became the guitarist in this. And they all turned up, and it was again like the concert in Toronto. I said – Will you come on? They said – Well, what are you going to play? You know. I said – Listen, we're going to do probably a Blues, or whatever was current, *Cold Turkey*, which is three chords, and Eric knew that. And *Don't Worry, Kyoko* which was Yoko's, which was three chords, a riff. I said once we get on to Yoko's riff, just keep hitting it. And it was a fantastic show. I don't think it was ever recorded. It was fantastic.

YOKO ONO: Very heavy.

JOHN LENNON: Very heavy.

ANDY PEEBLES: I think . . . I thought it was.

YOKO ONO: I thought it was . . . recorded.

JOHN LENNON: It was?

ANDY PEEBLES: It came out three years later on *Some Time In New York City*, did it not?

JOHN LENNON: Oh I'm sorry that . . . I'm not that clever . . .

YOKO ONO: *Some Time In New York City* was not that popular, because there was such a heavy piece . . .

JOHN LENNON: That was a heavy show, and a lot of the audience walked out, you know. But the ones that stayed, they were in a trance, man. They just all came to the front, because it was one of the first real heavy Rock shows, where we had a good, good band and that John and Yoko did together. And I always think that some of those kids – they were very young; it was a Unicef concert show – some of those kids formed those freaky bands later, because there were about two hundred kids at the front there, somewhere about thirteen, fourteen, fifteen, who were looking at Yoko and looking at us the way we were playing that *Don't Worry, Kyoko*, and it really reached a peak of whatever you call it. It really went out there that night. And I often think – I wonder if . . . you know, I hear touches of our early stuff in a lot of the Punk New Wave stuff. I could hear licks and flicks coming out. And I . . . it pleases me, it pleases both of us. I think . . . I bet . . . I'd love to know, were they in the audience? And did somebody go and form a group in London because it sounds . . . sure as hell sounds like it.

ANDY PEEBLES: It's an interesting thought. Eric Clapton was billed as Derek Claptoe, I think. This was sort of around the era when people had contractual problems I would imagine.

JOHN LENNON: The record companies always want to possess you mind, body and soul. You know, the record contracts always used to say any . . . anything you say they own too. You know. So all those BBC tapes that we did, officially EMI think they own them on a bit of paper, you know, I mean. Right. Every interview, every . . . everything.

ANDY PEEBLES: Right. December 1970, the *Plastic Ono Band* Album, which really did get some pretty good reviews, didn't it? And I think people . . .

JOHN LENNON: Yes. *The Mother*. We did a twin one . . . Yoko did one, and I did one. In fact, do you know what we were doing last night? We were playing Yoko's *Plastic Ono Band* Album. The first track is called *Why*. And it was the first real Rock 'n' Roll take we ever did together, and it's Ringo, Klaus, me on guitar, and Yoko on voice. And the fascinating thing is, even we didn't know where Yoko's voice started and where my guitar ended on the Intro. But you can tell. And we were playing it last night for . . . for Jack Douglas . . .

YOKO ONO: You know, it's something very strange, because, you know, John being what he is in a way, you know. Somehow he just goes all the way, so his guitar-playing in avant-garde was quite avant-garde really, you know, and we both suffered because people didn't appreciate what we were doing. But in fact John suffered as an avant-garde guitarist, and he was saying, Yeah, well I wish somebody would notice what I did, you know. And when you go back though, if anybody's interested, go back to Plastic Ono . . . Yoko and the *Plastic Ono Band* you know, that album, and his guitar-playing – somebody should notice it because it's just fantastic stuff.

JOHN LENNON: Thank you, mother. They will. We'll reissue them. (*Laughter*)

ANDY PEEBLES: Produced by John, Yoko and Phil Spector, if we stick on that for just a moment.

JOHN LENNON: Yeah, sure.

ANDY PEEBLES: And it was the first official solo LP.

JOHN LENNON: Yes. Yeah, yeah.

ANDY PEEBLES: So you were what you were at long last, and there were no strings attached, so to speak.

JOHN LENNON: Yes, it was . . . it was nice to do it, you know, and it was minimal again. I mean there was no over-dubbing. Just my guitar, a bass, and drums – or my piano, a bass and drums. And if you remember, at the beginning of *Mother*, the first . . . the beginning of the album has this bell going Dong . . . dong . . . dong . . . It's a church bell which I slowed down to thirty-three, so it's really like a horror movie, and that was like like the death knell of the Mother-Father Freudian trip. And if you listen to the beginning of *Double Fantasy*, you hear Ping . . . ping . . . ping . . .

ANDY PEEBLES: I was just thinking . . .

JOHN LENNON: Which is actually a bell that Yoko calls her Wishing Bell. You know, she rings the bell and makes a wish or whatever, which she can explain herself on that level; and I put it on to *Double Fantasy*, to show the likeness and the difference of the long, long trip from *Mother* to *Starting Over*.

ANDY PEEBLES: We'll be coming to that later. *Rolling Stone* gave it a five-star rating, that album, I seem to remember.

JOHN LENNON: Oh they did?

ANDY PEEBLES: And the critics said – 'Like all seminal rock, it's timeless in its concept'. Is that a sort of quote you appreciate?

JOHN LENNON: That's . . . well, it's better than Shit-head, or . . . (*Laughter*) I'm sorry. I don't know what you can say anymore in England. I hear all this – you can say anything on TV in England, and radio – I'm not sure. But also, it was reviewed as simplistic and self-indulgent.

YOKO ONO: No, I don't think so. Not simplistic, really? Oh all right.

JOHN LENNON: There was . . . I never forget a nasty word, my dear. Now self-indulgent means you talk about yourself, you know. So, as I was . . .

YOKO ONO: What else can you talk about?

JOHN LENNON: . . . again I was talking about this last night, I think. Because somebody said our film *Imagine* was self-indulgent. And then there was a remark that simplistic and self-indulgent to do with *Double Fantasy*. Now I've explained it somewhere and said – If we'd have used pseudonyms and called it *Tommy, the Rock Opera*, or created Ziggy Stardust and Sadie Glutz, and sang exactly the same lyrics as a third persona, then it's more acceptable to certain minds, you see. But because we don't put a persona on – I call it lipstick and clown make-up – we don't put a persona on, but we act . . . you can compare it with Method Acting say, when a Marlon Brando, or that ilk of actor, acts, they're themselves, but they're not themselves. Whereas, when Olivier acts, he becomes somebody else. Either one . . . I would not rate as, you know, this guy is better than that, or this person is better than that. But Marlon Brando could be called self-indulgent, and Olivier could be called not self-indulgent. To me, it's equal. We just prefer to not wear make-up, and use ourselves. But still there is a distance between what the records or the songs are saying and our real selves in our own privacy.

YOKO ONO: Well this is the sign when it's a very perverted society . . .

JOHN LENNON: Oh good . . .

YOKO ONO: . . . where directness, you know, is supposed to be something to be ashamed of, you know. So being directly yourself is something almost obscene, you know. I mean you have to somehow pretend that you are something other than yourself, you know. And that's not very . . .

JOHN LENNON: Interesting . . .

YOKO ONO: . . . interesting. So, well, we . . . I think we're direct by default in a way. You know. In other words, we just can't be anything else in a way. So we . . . so we are.

JOHN LENNON: I could be a cowboy. (*Laughter*)

ANDY PEEBLES: Phil Spector was involved there, John. I think somebody that you're pretty fond of, or . . .

JOHN LENNON: Yeah. I'm fond of his work a lot. His personality I don't . . . I'm not crazy about that, you know. But yeah, it was good to work with Phil, because I always admired him, and he contributed a lot. He contributed the Spector touch. But of course if you play John Lennon Plastic Ono, Yoko Ono Plastic Ono, because he's involved in both, and you play Phil Spector's work, you see there's a vast difference. We never gave him his head, you know, because we didn't let him go free on it. Otherwise he would be all things . . .

ANDY PEEBLES: Did he want . . . did he want it at the time?

JOHN LENNON: He always wants to. I mean he's got tremendous ego. He considers the artist like that film director considers actors, just pieces of garbage . . .

YOKO ONO: Canned goods.

JOHN LENNON: . . . canned goods that you bring on and you wheel off, you know. He'd like to bury the artist and so the production is the main thing. But we didn't allow him to do that to us. So on that level it was very good, because we used what we considered is . . . his amazing ear for pop music and sound, without letting it become (*deep voice*) Spector . . . you know, thousands of castanets . . .

ANDY PEEBLES: The wall of sound.

JOHN LENNON: The wall . . . we didn't want the wall of sound.

ANDY PEEBLES: No, no, right.

JOHN LENNON: But we wanted the outside input.

ANDY PEEBLES: *God's Song*. Critics said – 'Some of the finest of all rock-singing on the last verse' – I wonder where I got that from. I've got it written down.

JOHN LENNON: Who is this wonderful . . .

YOKO ONO: Thank you very much.

JOHN LENNON: Where is he when we need him? You know, who is he? I want to send him a card.

ANDY PEEBLES: We've been . . . I've been wending my way through some notes and that particular quote happened to come out.

JOHN LENNON: Oh that's right. That's the, I don't believe in . . .

YOKO ONO: I wish they had sent us personal notes about it, you know.

JOHN LENNON: Well, we've probably got it in our filing cabinet, you know.

YOKO ONO: Or something like . . .

ANDY PEEBLES: You have a filing cabinet?

JOHN LENNON: Oh we've got files on all the Press cuttings. Again, I don't know why we were discussing all this stuff last night, but we were. We were making that disco rock cut that we played to you earlier, which you can mention or not mention at your own choice. But, going back, and thinking what we were doing and what we'd done, and whether . . . You tend to remember the . . . the dig from a critic, rather than the praise, you see. That's why I'm looking at you . . . like . . . Somebody liked it? I had this impression that everybody hated the record, and that it was only regarded well about eight years later, when they . . . they'd started saying, Well, it's not as good as *Plastic Ono Band*, about the work I was doing later, you see.

ANDY PEEBLES: 1970 – as we move through – in February, *Instant Karma* – which was Top Five both here and in – or rather, I say Here, because we're here in America – but here in America and in Britain as well. And you actually appeared on *Top Of The Pops*. That was the first appearance by anybody connected with the Beatles for quite a while, wasn't it?

JOHN LENNON: It was great. I love being first. We were
talking about this last night – it's amazing.

ANDY PEEBLES: How did you feel about doing *Top Of The
Pops* after quite a time gap?

JOHN LENNON: Oh it was great. I love it, you know. I miss
the . . . again I was talking to Yoko about the Cavern today,
because there was two girls standing outside our apartment
today, and they'd been standing off and on for the last five
years, right through the so-called hiatus, you know, when I
wasn't . . . I was supposed to be buried alive, like Howard
Hughes. I'd talk to them, you know, and say, Hi, I said, I saw
you running across the park, and all that. And as we got in the
car I said to Yoko, you know this is like the Cavern; that's how
we communi . . . we were with the fans, you know, the . . .
they'd be at the door as we went in, at lunchtime, and they'd
say, Hey John, will you sing, you know, *Sweet Little Sixteen* for
Margie and Pam, you know. And it was on that level. I said
that's the kind of thing I miss, the direct communication where
you could talk to the audience. And you get in that sort of
Madison Square, Shea Stadium business, where you have to
over-act, you know. You have to act like eighteenth-century
actors of Grand Drama, which is not my schtik, and I like that
direct communication. That's why I like radio too. And I
enjoyed the *Instant Karma* thing because there were the
people right there. And we were talking about the fact that she
was knitting, you see. Because we did everything together.
Now she wasn't singing on *Instant Karma*. So I'm doing *Instant
Karma*, live – or it was a backing tape with live vocal, I think –
and she's just sitting there knitting this scarf, and there was
some review the next day – How dare she sit there knitting?
you know. But we wanted to be together, and her contribution
to that event, instead of having a smoke bomb or a coloured
light, a psychedelic light, Yoko only knitted. You see. And –
What are they doing? There's a film of that – I wish I could get
hold of it.

YOKO ONO: Knitting that goes nowhere in a way, you know.
Knitting is something very interesting. I mean it's almost like
sort of knitting a web or whatever, you know, a web of the

mind and all that, you know. There's something to it, really.

JOHN LENNON: It's a kind of meditation, I think, it's a . . .

ANDY PEEBLES: Yeah, I've tried it, and I'm a desperate failure. We won't go into that. I'm useless with a . . .

JOHN LENNON: I used to do embroidery. My auntie told me how to do little flowers, like that.

ANDY PEEBLES: *Mother* was released in fact in the United States of America, wasn't it, in 1971, as a single, but not in Britain.

JOHN LENNON: I don't know why. I can't remember why not. I probably didn't think it would make it as a single in England, that's all.

ANDY PEEBLES: Did you have total control over your products in those days, John?

YOKO ONO: Not really, no.

JOHN LENNON: Well, pretty much we decided what went out and what didn't go out, you know. We had to fight with the company all the time . . .

YOKO ONO: . . . that's true. No, we had to fight a little . . .

JOHN LENNON: . . . like the Live Peace thing, you know. They didn't want to put out . . . or they didn't like *Cold Turkey*. And they weren't too crazy, they didn't like the extra Beatle stuff. You know, they preferred to keep us in a box. So, but on the artistic level, yeah, we controlled it. I mean we took . . . we even made the covers ourselves, you know with Instamatic Cameras and Polaroids. The cover of *Imagine* Yoko took with Polaroid.

ANDY PEEBLES: I would imagine that having to fight, though, must be a tiring procedure mentally. I mean it must get very boring.

JOHN LENNON: It was.

YOKO ONO: Well it was sort of like an invisible fight, you know. They wouldn't really come out and say this and that. But it was sort of discouraged, in a very subtle way.

JOHN LENNON: *Two Virgins* was a big fight. That was like nine months later it came out. It was held up for nine months, you know. So Joseph Lockwood, you know, he was a nice, nice guy. But he sat down on a big table at the top of EMI with John and Yoko and told me he will do everything he can to help us.

YOKO ONO: To stop it.

JOHN LENNON: No, no, to help us, the first time.

YOKO ONO: Oh really? Oh.

JOHN LENNON: Yeah, you're not kidding? To help us put *Two Virgins* out, because we explained what it meant and why we were doing it. And he said he understood it and he'd do everything he can to help us. Then when we tried to put it out, he sent a personal note to everybody saying, Don't print it, don't put it out. You see. So we couldn't get the cover printed anywhere. It was really due out about nine months before it came out.

YOKO ONO: And it didn't come out as a Capitol record, you know. It was . . . Oh I think it came out as Tetra Gramophone or whatever.

JOHN LENNON: Yeah, over here, because we had to go with some other firm, you know. But now you can't get it for two hundred bucks.

ANDY PEEBLES: Now somebody told me this, when we came into this studio this morning actually, that the *Fly* album is going for thirty-five dollars at the moment. People are . . . she smiles when I say that.

JOHN LENNON: Yeah, down in the Village.

YOKO ONO: Yeah, I wish I had some. (*Laughter*)

JOHN LENNON: 1971, you were both resident in New York, and Yoko, I think you were going through problems because you were . . . you had a custody situation for your daughter. Is that right?

YOKO ONO: Yes.

ANDY PEEBLES: More pressure.

YOKO ONO: That's true, you know. I don't know how we survived. I mean we went through so many different kinds of pressure at that time.

ANDY PEEBLES: I mean the picture as I see it in front of me was that just when things were getting good, something else would rear its ugly head and maybe cause you a few mental problems.

YOKO ONO: But, you know, it was very strange, because we

40

were always having a dialogue and we were always sort of inspired by each other, and that kept us going, and also in a way I think that we were always giggling. (*Laughs*)

JOHN LENNON: Yeah, we tried to . . . you know . . . be. If we hadn't taken some of it with a pinch of salt, I think we would have both gone under, you know. I mean it was pretty hard. But usually one could sustain and support the other, but there were times when we both would go down, you know, and it's very hard, because the tendency is to go to drink or drugs, and it's very hard to get out then. But you can't when you're involved with legal court cases or immigration problems. One has to be right on the ball.

ANDY PEEBLES: Absolutely.

YOKO ONO: Oh I know, yes.

JOHN LENNON: But it might have done a lot of good, it might have done me harm. I can't really tell yet. You know, we seem to just go ploughing on any way producing it, but still I wonder how it would have been had we not been . . . you know, been harassed, but one cannot always blame everything on the outside, you know. Whatever happened to us was also partly our creation. And it was probably to do with complete self-involvement and not really taking care of business on an outside level and looking where we were going, you know, instead of looking where . . . down the road, we were always looking into each others' eyes. So I'm not . . . we're not taking the position that Society did everything to us.

YOKO ONO: No, no.

JOHN LENNON: And we take responsibility as well. I mean accidents happen and things do happen to you, but we do take some responsibility for the situation.

YOKO ONO: The custody fight is, you know, I mean we didn't have to go through that really and we shouldn't have done it on a level of court case, you know, and whatnot, but at the same time on hindsight at least Kyoko would remember that we were interested in her, you know.

ANDY PEEBLES: And that's very important.

YOKO ONO: . . . so that's like a by-product, you know.

JOHN LENNON: We still don't know where they are . . .

41

ANDY PEEBLES: . . . really?

JOHN LENNON: . . . oh no we haven't seen hide nor hair of them. She has a piece of paper saying custody, that's it.

ANDY PEEBLES: Incredible situation.

JOHN LENNON: Yes.

YOKO ONO: But so many things that have happened to us are so incredible that we just couldn't help; I mean we just had to say to each other isn't this amazing, you know, and just laugh about it, there's nothing we can do about it, you know.

JOHN LENNON: It was like a Pinter play, you know, only we were in it, never ending.

YOKO ONO: This is what I mean, you know.

ANDY PEEBLES: March '71, I keep pulling out these dates because they're important – *Power To The People*, another one to add to the collection, any memories of that now? It's not that long ago really, but it's nine years, as we sit here on this December day in 1980. Does it seem a helluva long time ago to you?

JOHN LENNON: Oh it just seems like *Power To The People*, wasn't that the First World War, no it wasn't. I remember that that was the expression going round those days and that I'd just . . . Tariq Ali had kept coming round wanting money for the *Red Mole* or some magazine or other and I used to give anybody – it was sort of Left Field, avant-garde or sort of in the Art field or political field – money kind of out of guilt, as well, because I was thinking, well, I'm working class and I am not one of them, but I am rich so therefore I have to; so anytime anybody said something like that, I would fork out, you know, and he was hustling for whatever he was hustling for and I kind of wrote *Power To The People* in a way kind of as a guilt song, you know, so I thought I'd better do that, you know.

YOKO ONO: But incidentally we heard it last night just by accident so to speak, and it's very heavy, very good.

JOHN LENNON: Yeah, not bad, to me it's like a newspaper song, you know, when you write about something instant that's going on right now and I don't call it a well-crafted song or anything, just that was the news headline with misprints and everything but the B side was *Open Your Box* which is worth a

42

play, Yoko Ono in all her finery.

YOKO ONO: And which was banned at the time.

JOHN LENNON: Again it was banned in America, because box in America means something to do with the female anatomy below the waist.

ANDY PEEBLES: Beautifully put, sir, beautifully put. We move to *Imagine* in 1971. John, it wasn't released as a single until November 1975, that's a four-year gap and I think if you said to most . . .

YOKO ONO: I can't believe it really.

ANDY PEEBLES: . . . really and if you were to say to most music programmers around the world, which would be the John Lennon track they would instantly pick to play, I think it would be *Imagine*, it's had fantastic airplay.

JOHN LENNON: Amazing, it was made in '72 and put out in '75?

ANDY PEEBLES: November 1971 you did the *Imagine* Album and it was released in November 1975 eventually as a single. And I remember trying to find it on a single, I think you could get it on American import for a while but eventually, I think I'm right in saying Great Britain finally decided to do something with it and put it out as a single.

JOHN LENNON: I must say I'm blank on why that would have happened, it must have been either because Klein and EMI or whoever was . . .

YOKO ONO: Decided it was a bit too political.

JOHN LENNON: Too political or it'll sell the album better or whatever reasoning they had because it was a single in America, I believe, and I think it was something to do with . . .

YOKO ONO: . . . yes that's right.

JOHN LENNON: . . . they wanted to sell the album so make 'em buy the album to get it . . . some garbage like that it surprises me, well actually that should be credited as a Lennon/Ono song, a lot of it – the lyric and the concept – came from Yoko, but those days I was a bit more selfish, a bit more macho and I sort of omitted to mention her contribution, but it was right out of *Grapefruit*, her book, there's a whole pile of pieces about imagine this and imagine that and I have given her credit now long overdue.

YOKO ONO: Well, I mean everything we did together in those days we just inspired each other, so you know there's that, it's hard not to get inspired.

JOHN LENNON: Yeah, but if it had been Bowie I would have put Lennon/Bowie if it had been a male, you know, when we wrote *Fame* together I wrote . . . did something with Harry Nilsson, *Old Dirt Road*, as Lennon/Nilsson, but when we did it I just put Lennon, because, you know, she's just the wife and, you know, you don't put her name on, right?

YOKO ONO: Well, that's before *Woman Is The Nigger Of The World*. I suppose I'm coming to that.

ANDY PEEBLES: We are coming to that, yes, indeed.

JOHN LENNON: Up to the next banned record, right?

ANDY PEEBLES: Before we get to it, I have to say that on that *Imagine* album there is a track called *How do you Sleep?* which other people considered was a swing at Mr McCartney.

JOHN LENNON: Well, I think I explained it pretty well in a *Playboy* interview that I used my resentment against Paul that I have as a kind of sibling rivalry resentment from youth, to create a song.

ANDY PEEBLES: Does it go back that far?

JOHN LENNON: Oh yeah, I mean rivalry between two guys I mean it's, it was always there, it was a creative rivalry, like there was a rivalry between the Beatles and the Stones, it was a creative rivalry. In that respect it was not a terrible vicious, horrible vendetta because it's not on that level, but one tends when interviewed by a print press . . . see now you can hear the tone of my voice, so I can say I felt resentment against . . .

ANDY PEEBLES: I can see the face too.

JOHN LENNON: Right, you can see the face too, and know what I'm saying is . . . I felt resentment so I used that situation the same as I used withdrawing from heroin to write *Cold Turkey*. I used my resentment and withdrawing from Paul and the Beatles and the relationship with Paul to write *How do you Sleep?* I don't really, you know . . . go around with those thoughts in my head all the time, I wanted to make a funky track and this is a good way to make it.

YOKO ONO: Well, I remember when he was writing, he was a

44

bit tongue in cheek, you know, oh wait till they see this.

JOHN LENNON: Oh we were laughing . . . and we got the line . . .

YOKO ONO: And it wasn't out of anger in a way, so it was inspiration was a tiny bit of it.

JOHN LENNON: It's like Klein gave me *Another Day*, I was saying what is it what is it and he said, what about *Another Day*? And I said, you're just another day because that was some single he had. . . . laughing about mine, you know, but in print it looks terrible if I comment about it in like *Rolling Stone* or *Playboy*, it looks like I'm freaking out about him like Dr Jekyll or something, it's not that at all.

ANDY PEEBLES: Right, in '72 the deportation case (*John Lennon sings opening bar of* Dragnet) . . .

YOKO ONO: Can you imagine all this – I mean it's incredible.

JOHN LENNON: What a life – it'd make a movie.

YOKO ONO: I can't believe it, that two people, two very naïve . . .

ANDY PEEBLES: As I sit here talking to you, I'm finding it hard to believe you have been through a lot. You really have been through a lot.

YOKO ONO: Boys and girls.

JOHN LENNON: Through the mill.

ANDY PEEBLES: But Mayor Lindsay in New York did a lot of things on your behalf, did he not, round about that era?

JOHN LENNON: He was very good to us and he said lots of things like, you know, we should welcome artists to our shores because this is the haven, isn't it? It's got the big iron lady [Statue of Liberty] out in the sea there saying welcome to the shore and they were trying to kick me out: it's ridiculous when you look back on it, because the most I could have done was gather a big gang of, you know, demonstrators together which the police could have shot, so what are they complaining about?

YOKO ONO: When we did the Bed-In in Toronto, was it that? There was a specific instruction, I understand, from the government to the Press, the American Press, that they should not put us on the front page because they did initially when we did the Bed-In; so I think that we were thinking that our Peace and Love movement was very subversive but, in fact, the government was very aware of it, it seems like, you know, they caught on, you know, maybe the people didn't catch on.

JOHN LENNON: We were the kind of the court jesters of the youth movement.

ANDY PEEBLES: Did you see yourselves really as the court jesters of the youth movement?

JOHN LENNON: Well, now I do, looking back, you know, because we tried to do it with humour. It was really irrelevant what sort of serious critics in the pop business said about what we were doing in bed and bags, and that as long as our – what we felt our duty or our position was – to keep on about peace, until something happened, you know, and it was in the tradition of Gandhi, only with a sense of humour.

ANDY PEEBLES: June 1972, *Some Time in New York City* which we referred to a little bit earlier on, because it included the live side and it was a collaboration between the two of you and Elephant's Memory, Phil Spector was involved, Frank Zappa was involved as well.

JOHN LENNON: Yeah, because he was appearing in the Fillmore – some dance hall in New York, famous one.

ANDY PEEBLES: The Fillmore East?

YOKO ONO: The Fillmore, yeah.

JOHN LENNON: Yeah, and we bumped into him, and he said, Will you come down and jam with us? So we thought, Great, we'll just go down, we'd just come from London a couple . . . about a week before or something, we went down there and I did an old Olympics number – the B side of *Young Blood* – I'm not sure what it was called. Well, it was a 12-bar kind of thing that I used to do at the Cavern, it was the B side of some hit American record and Yoko did – Yoko, which one did you do?

YOKO ONO: I don't remember.

JOHN LENNON: Well it was something mad anyway, and it was pretty good with Zappa because he's pretty 'far out' as they say, so we blended quite well, so it was a combination of sort of mad rock and new, what I consider newspaper style writing of songs of what was currently going on like Attica State or *Woman Is The Nigger* or whatever the . . .

46

YOKO ONO: But it was really like Bertolt Brecht, you know, I mean the style of writing was, you know, and I thought it was pretty interesting theatre, you know. That's what I think . . .

JOHN LENNON: Well, that's what I had . . . because you took me to see that play didn't you, *Threepenny Opera*.

YOKO ONO: Yeah, it's like that, but then also in the classical field I'm sure people would understand it but I mean somehow in the pop field they thought well, you know, but the cover, the record cover we had Chairman Mao and Nixon naked dancing together and, of course, I mean this was the sort of thing we had to fight for; I thought it was great, but then without telling us they put a little, what is it, a sales stamp or something on top of it.

JOHN LENNON: But you couldn't even steam it off, so they wouldn't have Nixon and Mao dancing naked together, you know.

YOKO ONO: And that was our record company doing that to us, you know.

JOHN LENNON/YOKO ONO: To us, you know, without telling us, you know.

JOHN LENNON: Kids were writing into us and complaining that they'd go to the supermarket, wherever you buy 'em, buy the record, and then they'd try and get this label, saying the latest or some sales hype on it, and you couldn't get it off, it ripped the cover to shreds, just petty, petty crap. They could have covered it without ruining it so as when you got home you could unveil it, but what the hell, I mean, you couldn't see any pubic hair, it was just two bodies we just stuck, she, it was her idea, she just stuck their two heads on and it was hysterical, but you can't see it now, eebahgum.

YOKO ONO: Because, you know, sense of humour was part of our, you know, like John says, but also I really think it's interesting that they started by then, the record company I think was very nervous because they felt that we were being so controversial and all that, you know, and so they really started to do that. It's interesting that they were so nervous, you know.

ANDY PEEBLES: Can I talk to you about *Woman Is The Nigger Of The World*, Yoko?

YOKO ONO: Umm well, what about it?

ANDY PEEBLES: Tell me about it and how it came to be.

YOKO ONO: Well, you see the thing was, well I have to be honest about it, I mean, you know, in New York I was an artist and I was sort of doing my own thing and I was pretty sort of free and then I went to London and I was doing these gallery shows and whatnot, concerts and all that, then I met John and then right smack sort of – I was putting this sort of suggestion you know . . . for men who are from Liverpool and their lot or whatever they are from Liverpool and this was the first experience in the place of what is it, I would say it was the first experience because – no that's not true – but . . .

JOHN LENNON: Get on, get on.

YOKO ONO: I felt, you know, it was sort of big machoism, you know, and nothing to do with their songs, I mean their songs were so beautiful, but as people, you know, what is this, what is this? I was really sort of naïve about it all, you know, in a way. Though in New York I must say I was an artist I did confront a homosexual mafia kind of suggestion of where, you know, the art world was controlled by homosexuals, gay people shall we say . . .

JOHN LENNON: Happy-go-luckier than we are.

YOKO ONO: Yeah, all right, of those days and there was that, but I didn't feel it that much really and this was time it was sort of like a personal situation and I started to feel, well, I mean, what are we going to do for instance . . .

JOHN LENNON: We did the interview with *Nova*.

YOKO ONO: D'you wanna?

JOHN LENNON: No, go on, go on.

YOKO ONO: It's all right?

JOHN LENNON: Yes.

YOKO ONO: So we did an interview in *Nova* and when I think I was asked some questions and all that I just well, you know, um Woman Is The Nigger Of The World and that was quoted on *Nova* cover or something.

JOHN LENNON: Which is a dead magazine, it was a magazine in England at the time like *Vogue* or something.

YOKO ONO: Well, because you see like breakfast table or

48

something, they said we have a morning paper and I was just sort of – start naturally the papers and John would say, oh well what because he was used to looking at the paper first.

JOHN LENNON: Don't take the paper till Dad's read it, you know.

ANDY PEEBLES: Sunday Morning Blues.

JOHN LENNON: You'll not touch papers till Dad has it, you know, slippers and pipe.

YOKO ONO: You know, what is this I am not supposed to read the papers first, you know, I couldn't believe it, you know, just on that kind of . . .

ANDY PEEBLES: Unwritten English law.

YOKO ONO: You know, on a trivial level but all these things accumulate, you know, and that's why I was inspired to say Woman is the Nigger of the World. I mean, you know, directly inspired by life with . . .

JOHN LENNON: Knew how to treat a Nigger like. Well anyway I took the title and wrote the song *Woman Is The Nigger Of The World* which I believe was long before Helen Reddy's *I Am Woman.* So it was the first Woman's Liberation song as well, as far as I'm concerned, and it was directly quoted from her but her singing it probably would have not got on the air. But she did do *Sisters Oh Sisters* which we did reggae on the B side. It turned out to be the B side but I remember that session because Elephant's Memory, all New York kids, you know, saying they didn't know what reggae was, I'm trying to trying to explain to them all, the only lick I knew to teach them was *The Israelites*, that Desmond Dekker thing – so if you listen to it you'll hear me going trying to get them to reggae, ten years later they write to me saying, Oh we understand reggae now, any work? you know, screw you kid, it's too much hard work, you know what I mean?

ANDY PEEBLES: *Woman Is The Nigger Of The World.*

JOHN LENNON: That was banned in America again because you couldn't say nigger.

YOKO ONO: The word nigger.

JOHN LENNON: Although our good friend and old, old friend Dick Gregory helped us by getting us in the black magazines called *Ebony* and there's one other which I've forgotten the name of, and posing with pictures of us with a lot of black guys stood up and women and said, We understand what he's saying, We are not offended, but the ones who were offended were the honky whites so that wasn't played on the air either, you could never hear it. *Ballad of John and Yoko*, by the way, was banned over here. So what they did was turn the word, they don't like the word Christ, you know, unless you're wearing a white robe you can't say Christ here, so they turned it round so that it would, you know, it ain't easy, you know, so that's how they fixed that one. And *Woman Is The Nigger* – we were on a TV talk show – Dick Cavett show which is like a kind of Eamonn Andrews, I don't know who is the current in England now . . .

ANDY PEEBLES: Michael Parkinson and Russell Harty.

JOHN LENNON: Hullo Mike, how are you? Manchester! So anyway, Granada he used to be.

ANDY PEEBLES: . . . he did . . .

JOHN LENNON: Right so he, Dick Cavett, had this national TV show and he was willing to let us sing it because he was a liberal, you know, quote unquote, and the company had a big hullaballoo backstage and we did manage to do it live on his show once but the hullaballoo was amazing. I mean, it was like I'd trodden on the flag or something. Now doesn't it look silly? Isn't it incredible?

ANDY PEEBLES: But the situations that you have talked about begin to look silly in retrospect as you look backwards now, don't they?

JOHN LENNON: It's just absolutely ridiculous but when you think it's such a beautiful statement, you know, what she was saying is true, woman still is the nigger – there's only one, you can talk about blacks, you can talk about Jews, you can talk about the Third World, you can talk about everything but underlying that whole thing, under the whole crust of it is the women and beneath them children, as Dick Gregory said to us in 1969 in Denmark, 'Children's liberation is the next movement'. Because they have no rights whatsoever, absolutely none, women have a certain amount but children is the next thing – children power – but the women will liberate the children.

YOKO ONO: Well, you know, just the other day Sean was coming to me and he was very serious and he's five years old, you know, and he said, 'Mummy, you know, when you say something they take it seriously but when I say something they don't believe me'.

JOHN LENNON: Yeah he said that.

YOKO ONO: Well, I said I'm very sorry but that's how it is, you know, and grown-ups we don't understand, you know, and it's bad you know.

ANDY PEEBLES: December 1972 – *Happy Christmas War is Over* – which will doubtless be played hundreds of times on British, maybe American, Radio.

JOHN LENNON: Yeah, they do play it here, thank God.

ANDY PEEBLES: But they do play it in Britain as well, John, they do play it an awful lot, and I'm as guilty as the next disc jockey.

JOHN LENNON: We're very proud of that one and we both played and sang together on that one . . . might have been our first pop, you know, straight pop record together and Phil was the producer and it was a beautiful session and the kids singing were beautiful . . .

ANDY PEEBLES: The Harlem Community Choir was it not?

JOHN LENNON: Yeah, it was a really nice pleasant thing and basically I said to Phil, give me the backing you gave to George on a thing that George wrote for Ronnie Spector – and it's slipped my mind now, which is *Try Some Buy Some* – if you want to do some comparison shopping and listen to the track *Try Some Buy Some* that George has made with Ronnie Spector or whatever, you'll hear the idea for the backing there which is what we did. As usual, we messed it up, we recorded it a bit too late, we almost missed the Christmas market that year with that record.

ANDY PEEBLES: It got to Number Four in Britain.

JOHN LENNON: I think we almost got it out earlier in Britain than we did in America, something held us up, I can't remember, there were so many things going on but what we wanted to do was have something besides *White Christmas* being played every Christmas, you know, and there's always a war, right, there's always somebody getting shot, so every year you can play it and there's always somebody being tortured or shot somewhere, so the lyric stands in that respect.

ANDY PEEBLES: There's also, for some strange reason, in Britain an incredible fight to get the Number One record at Christmas for years.

JOHN LENNON: Well, it's the same here.

ANDY PEEBLES: Joyously orientated or just by whoever it happens to be, but I've always found that very, very strange . . .

JOHN LENNON: Yeah, yeah, but I've always wanted to write something that would be a Christmas record that would last forever you know, maybe that's not the one maybe . . .

YOKO ONO: We should reissue it.

JOHN LENNON: Well, I hope they reissue it forever, but also we did the poster event which is also – *War Is Over If You Want It.*

ANDY PEEBLES: You might be interested to know that every Christmas since you released that single, I've received a new copy, every year, wherever I've been broadcasting.

JOHN LENNON: Oh fantastic, I wish they'd send us one, I don't even have one.

ANDY PEEBLES: My producer, Paul Williams, and myself have had a copy each this Christmas as indeed we did last year and the year before.

JOHN LENNON: What do they put on the other side?

YOKO ONO: That's beautiful.

ANDY PEEBLES: Now you've got me, now you've got me.

JOHN LENNON: That would be fascinating, maybe they'd put it on both sides, you know, the DJ copy kind of stuff.

ANDY PEEBLES: But it comes round every year.

JOHN LENNON: Great, isn't that great?

ANDY PEEBLES: It's a little something you didn't know here in the USA.

JOHN LENNON: I want to say something while it's in my mind because we keep talking about Plastic Ono Band, Plastic Ono Band. Plastic Ono Band was a concept of Yoko's which is an imaginary band. The first advert for the Plastic Ono Band was a photograph of some pieces of plastic with a tape recorder and a TV in it, because they didn't have this great material that they have now, you know, lasers and lights and machines that can do all this stuff. And her idea was that a completely robot pop group – that was what she must have thought of us all when she first came into the world – because she immediately said, Oh I've got an idea, this band. And the first advert was a page out of the London Telephone Book of the Jones's, this was in the *NME* and all the papers, you know, and pictures of these plastic things. And there was supposed to be a party for the release of the *Give Peace a Chance* record which was the first Plastic Ono Band record, but we'd had a car crash or something so we couldn't come; so at the dance hall where they had the party for the Plastic Ono Band all the Press came to meet the band and the band was on stage which was just a machine with a camera pointing at them showing them on the stage themselves.

So the Plastic Ono Band is a conceptual band that never was, there never had been any members of it and the advert said, You are the Plastic Ono Band. So I just want to clear that, it wasn't the reforming a new band like a Wings or a Hollies, or whatever, where you have a name and you belong to it, there's nobody ever been in that band, there are no members. While I was telling this wonderful story ladies and gentlemen, Yoko's putting a fur coat on and Paul Williams is writing messages on the mike, so you can hear the pen and the paper rattling, you see.
YOKO ONO: That's the accompaniment . . .
JOHN LENNON: Oh, I see.
YOKO ONO: . . . it's the music accompaniment.
THEY AGREE ON A BREAK AND CHAT TOGETHER . . .

ANDY PEEBLES: November 1973 and the *Mind Games* Album, John?
JOHN LENNON: Ah, this is the BBC World Service!
ANDY PEEBLES: You do that well, you do that well.
JOHN LENNON: I was listening I told you before, Bermuda, Singapore, Cape Town. And may I just comment on that?
ANDY PEEBLES: Please do . . .

JOHN LENNON: . . . that I read the papers when the PM Margaret Thatcher was going to cut the BBC World Service down, that would be the greatest disservice to peace, love and understanding in the world because one, you really appreciate it and every country does, that you don't know how important it is that the English speaking, our point of view, our way of life, we in the West and our whole ideals are presented by the BBC and they're the only ones that can do it – the Americans don't have the system, they don't have the contacts in all the countries because they didn't have the Commonwealth and the Empire. And from India to Cape Town to everywhere – it would be a great disservice to the world if it was cut down. I believe that they did allow it to stay but . . .

ANDY PEEBLES: Yes they did.

JOHN LENNON: . . . but that would be . . . better to sell off some of the Church property and finance the radio, or something, you know, whatever it is because it's very important, and people appreciate it all over and not just English people living abroad, or whites living in Australia, but all the races on earth listen to that and it's very important because I travel and listen, I hear it, I talk to people about it and everybody's listening. So *Mind Games*.

ANDY PEEBLES: The BBC World Service.

JOHN LENNON: Yeah, *Mind Games* is what they're playing with the world and they have to keep it up.

ANDY PEEBLES: 1973, it's only seven years ago now, isn't it?

JOHN LENNON: Yeah, we're getting closer.

ANDY PEEBLES: We're getting closer, it's another one of your much-played tracks actually, the title track of *Mind Games*, isn't it?

JOHN LENNON: Oh that's good. That was a fun track because the voice is in stereo and the seeming orchestra on it is just me playing three notes with a slide guitar. (*Sings*) And the middle eight is reggae. Trying again to explain to American musicians what reggae was in 1973 was pretty hard, but it's basically a reggae middle eight if you listen to it. (*Sings*) But it was hard telling these, you know, they didn't know what reggae was then. I'm glad it's played, it ain't bad.

54

ANDY PEEBLES: Do you follow what's played of your material on American Radio? . . . because here we are in New York, I've been listening a lot to American Radio and found it very interesting. Are you an avid radio listener? You've just mentioned the World Service, so obviously you do listen to radio, what about music radio?

JOHN LENNON: Well, for a long time I wasn't listening to music because, to the pop radio, you know, to the rock 'n' roll stuff, because it would either cause me to get sweaty, you know, because it would bring back memories I didn't want to know about or I would get that feeling that I'm not alive because I'm not making it. And if it was good I hated it because I wasn't doing it, if it was bad I was furious because I could have done better, so whatever, so I didn't get involved and I listened to classical and muzak and stuff like that mainly, for five years, but now once I've started tuning in again to pop of course I'm on the dial all the time. I have a TV on with no sound and play the radio mainly.

YOKO ONO: And just for feminists in England, I'm sure of . . .

JOHN LENNON: Both of them.

ANDY PEEBLES: There are a lot.

YOKO ONO: But while John made *Imagine* I made *Approximately Universe* and when John was making *Mind Games* I made a record called *Feeling in Space* and both albums are full of feminist songs, songs of woman. So . . .

ANDY PEEBLES: Can you define a feminist, Yoko? As you would like to see one.

YOKO ONO: Well, John is a feminist.

JOHN LENNON: Aaah.

YOKO ONO: Anybody who's aware of woman's struggle and what they have to go through in the male society.

ANDY PEEBLES: Do you have specific feminists whom you personally admire?

YOKO ONO: Well, I mean, I admire all women because they're all basically feminists, but, at the same time, I mean, something like in America that there are many feminist men starting to be aware of the feminist movement and all that, and I really appreciate that and also, I mean, it's harder for men to become feminist of course but they are aware of the woman's movement as part of the social structure and social movement, and I think that part is the most interesting because in the end we have to really come together and work together about it. And I don't think without men's co-operation in the end it's not going to work.

ANDY PEEBLES: And I ought to say that during that period you two went through a bit of a break-up didn't you?

JOHN LENNON: Yeah, I call it my lost weekend, it lasted eighteen months when the feminist side of me died slightly and she said, Get the Hell out and kicked me out.

ANDY PEEBLES: And you took to jumping out of cars, I've been reading.

JOHN LENNON: Just the once.

ANDY PEEBLES: . . . it was only once.

JOHN LENNON: Well, I was pretty self-destructive at college too, when I went to art school in Liverpool, you know, it was mainly one long drinking session, but when you're eighteen/ nineteen you can put away a lot of drink and not hurt your body so much. But what I did when she kicked me out was I hit the bottle like I was eighteen or nineteen, when you're thirty whatever, thirty-seven or whatever I was when that happened, I don't know – whatever I was, you can't take as much booze but I was acting like I was still at college, you know, just wacking it out and just going out all the time. And I remember at college I always got a little violent on drink but somehow, I used to have a friend called Jeff Mohammed, rest his soul, who died, he was a half Indian Arab who was my friend at art school. He would be like a bodyguard for me, so whenever I'd get into some controversy, he would sort of ease me out of it. But I do recall at college punching through telephone box glass, you see, so it was a kind of self-destructive suicide side of me which is resolving itself for the better I believe, as I get older, because I never enjoyed it, you know. I don't like that waking up and thinking what happened – did I kill somebody? I mean the Beatles first national coverage was me beating up Bob Wooller, at Paul's twenty-first party because he intimated I was homosexual. I must have had a fear that maybe I was homosexual to attack him like that and it's very complicated reasoning. But I was very drunk and I hit him and I could have really killed somebody then. And that scared me. Paul was twenty-one so I must have been twenty-three then and that was in the *Daily Mirror*, it was the back page, I remember the picture. It was a posed picture – a Beatle posed on the docks picture – but it was pretty scary and it was the kind of re-hash of my youth. But of course acting like a teenager in Hollywood in public with the Press. You see what I could, would do as an individual in Liverpool would not go in the *Liverpool Echo* right, but when I would do something dumb like put a Kotex on my head in a restaurant, it becomes a national story, or, you know, take a pee in the wrong place or something then it becomes a great, great event. But it damaged, it was a very unhealthy period for me but I couldn't deal with the separation any other way. I mean you know I just fell apart and the only thing I knew was go to the bar and drink.

ANDY PEEBLES: Which you did with a gentleman called Harry Nilsson.

JOHN LENNON: Harry Nilsson and poor old Keith Moon and various others. Ringo, who is not unknown to tipple a few himself, and it was a pretty hectic period, pretty wild and it sounds funny in retrospect but it was pretty miserable, yeah, pretty bad period – and I'm thankful that I'm out of it and I don't drink now because it scares me, you know even a glass of wine knocks me out now, so I'm happy about that, forget about the booze.

ANDY PEEBLES: *Walls and Bridges* came along in 1974. It's said that you wrote the ten songs in a period of a week to get that album together, is that true?

JOHN LENNON: I did. I dunno, it's all a blank. I probably did, yeah, it might sound like that too – I don't know.

ANDY PEEBLES: I want to ask you about writing, I mean ten songs in a week is a lot of pressure, how do you go about writing, John, these days . . .? Because we'll be coming up to *Double Fantasy* in the not too distant future. Or the both of you as a combination, which is more important.

JOHN LENNON: Looking back at it, whenever I comment about

writing, I always seem to have been suffering, whether it was writing *Day in the Life* or whatever, you know, when I comment about it, everything is like some kind of suffering. I always seem to have an intense time writing and thinking this is the end and nothing's coming and this is dumb and how can I, you know, this is no good and all that business. So not writing for the five years which I didn't, I didn't pick up a guitar or anything and not trying to write, not making an attempt to write or anything like that, so what you said about *Walls and Bridges* applies to *Double Fantasy*. I was in Bermuda and Yoko was in New York doing some business. I was in Bermuda with Sean and the Nanny so . . . and when we made a tentative decision to come when the month was over in Bermuda . . . that we would make a record, I didn't have any material. Then suddenly it all came to me, all the songs that are on *Double Fantasy* all came in a period of three weeks in Bermuda after five years of nothing. Not trying but nothing coming anyway, no inspiration, no thought, no anything, then suddenly voom voom voom.

YOKO ONO: It hit both of us, but our sort of inspired writers, shall we say, that when he writes or I did that too . . .

JOHN LENNON: You never stop.

YOKO ONO: (*Laughs*) But I mean he's a very fast writer, because it's an inspiration, it's just comes to him so it's just a matter of writing it down almost and so when we did *Double Fantasy* I was in New York, he was in Bermuda, we would sort of communicate on the phone and I would say, well what about this, you know? And then he would call me, maybe four hours later, you know, what about this? Be singing to each other and that was the dialogue, very strange, you know? And we went through sort of like . . . paradoxical feeling of half-resisting, you know, well I don't want to hear a song now, I'm very tired or you know . . . but I, well, I mean, I've heard yours, all right well, let's hear it then, you know, that sort . . . I went through that. And then we were going to go to studio and because of that I felt well, you know . . . we worked together . . . it's going to be like we're both pig-headed people and so maybe we're going to fight like crazy over remix or this and that because we both have very definite ideas. I'm sure that John thought that way too, John must have thought well, can we really work together, you know? And it's after five years of not working . . . there's that too, but somehow it was really surprising, I mean, you know, it's almost like people, like, feel disappointed hearing this business, so it's too good to be true, but somehow we were so well. And we were all prepared to maybe have a difficult time but don't you think . . .?

JOHN LENNON: Yeah, it was the easiest set I've ever done, I think.

ANDY PEEBLES: Five years is an awful long time. What sort of mental discipline did it involve resisting picking up a guitar?

JOHN LENNON: Well, it wasn't a matter of resisting. The first half year or year that I had this sort of feeling in the back of my mind that I ought to, and I'd go through periods of panic when . . . because I was not in the *NME* or the *Billboard* or being seen at Studio 54 with Mick and Bianca . . . I mean, you know, just I didn't exist anymore. I got a little fear of that, would come like a paranoia, then it would go away because I'd be involved with the baby or involved with whatever sort of business that we were involved with. But that only lasted about nine months, and then there was suddenly like a 'oh!' it just went away, and I realised there was a life after death, you know, there was a life without it.

ANDY PEEBLES: Did you enjoy that realisation?

JOHN LENNON: It was great, it was like, oh my God, and I would sit around thinking what does this remind me of, what does this remind me of, what does this remind me of? It reminds me of being fifteen. I didn't have to write songs at fifteen, I wrote if I wanted to but played rock 'n' roll if I wanted to. I didn't have to do it, I didn't have some imaginary standard set up by me or by some group of critics or whatever.

ANDY PEEBLES: In other words back to days before the pressure started?

JOHN LENNON: Yes. So it was before, I sort of got back to that and that's when I suddenly could do it again with ease. The most enjoyable thing for me, apart from putting them on the tape when you first put them, is the inspirational, in the spirit, that, because when the songs really come and you're not sitting

down like a craftsman writing. I can do that, you know. You
want a song about bananas for a movie? I could do that, okay
I'm quite capable of turning it out like that – I wouldn't enjoy
it so much maybe – but I could do it on that level. But my joy
is when you're like possessed, like a medium, you know.
I'll be sitting round and it'll come in the middle of the night or
at the time when you don't want to do it – that's the exciting
part.

So I'm lying around and then this thing comes as a whole
piece, you know, words and music, and I think well, you know,
can I say I wrote it? I don't know who the hell wrote it – I'm just
sitting here and this whole damned song comes out. So it,
you're like driven and you find yourself over on a piano or
guitar and you put it down because it's been given to you or
whatever it is that you tune into.

ANDY PEEBLES: How did you find him during this period,
Yoko?

YOKO ONO: Yes, he was doing that and, of course, I was doing
that too, we are very similar that way, you know, so when it
comes, it comes, so it sort of comes in bunches, you know,
and . . .

ANDY PEEBLES: But were you relieved that he had finally
decided to lay down the guitar and rest?

YOKO ONO: Well, I mean, we weren't suffering or we weren't
feeling worried when we were just relaxing so there was no,
you know, strong feeling really. In fact, the nicest thing about
Double Fantasy was that while we were making it, we were
fully aware that we didn't have to make it. We were making it
and enjoying it, but we could always go back to the other life
because the thing was that we now know that we have the other
life as well. It's not like we always have to be in the front, you
know.

JOHN LENNON: Yeah, so that was the joy of if, it's the same joy
now, had it not been accepted – by now it has been well
accepted here in England and America and various parts north
and south of the world – but if it hadn't, I would have been, we
would have been hurt, you know, and, you know, whatever
one would feel – but then one wouldn't have wanted to have

60

killed oneself or, you know, get . . . go back to the bottle because somebody didn't like your record or whatever. So knowing that gives you a kind of freedom that you have when you're younger, when you sort of don't have a past to live up to and that's the joy of it. I have a past but I don't have to live up to it.

ANDY PEEBLES: Were your friends very surprised that you adopted that stance as far as taking the five years off was concerned? I mean, was there any external pressure which people put on you and said, come on John, what's happening?

JOHN LENNON: There was a lot . . . that's why, you remember when you asked me, I think it was off-mike, before we started, you know, have you got any English friends in town . . .? Well, suddenly when Mick Jagger or David Bowie or Elton John came to town I wouldn't respond, you know, because they'd always want me to go down to the studio or to the clubs and I didn't want to get in there again . . . or Harry Nilsson you know . . . it's like birds of a feather. So I didn't want to go back in that pressure part of my life again. I wasn't ready to do that and there was pressure from friends like that, you know, and Mick did this whole spiel in *The Observer* in London which I read in Tokyo, because we spent half the first three years of Sean's life, like half the early seventies in Japan, six, seven, eight months at a time, and I got this version of it in Tokyo where Mick was saying, 'Come on, John, get out of there'. Everyone was sort of on my case, as they say, saying how dare I not be doing it. You know, what's it got to do with Mick whether I'm not doing it, all the rock stars were commenting on what I was not doing, you know, I couldn't understand them. I thought, well, how square of them, how dumb. He's going on about hiding behind your kid, you know, he was trying to be nice about it – he wasn't attacking me but it was a sort of little edge to it. He said, I like John very much but he's hiding behind Sean, and why doesn't he get his finger out, and Yoko's got him locked up. I know what that's like, what that is like, don't kid me that you're doing it for the family, because you can have both. Well, you know, he lived to learn that lesson because he didn't have both, okay, and that was before he split with Bianca and the child and all that, which I feel sorry for him about. The pain that one goes through – separation and having a child involved – but I didn't feel as though I could have both and it was more important to have a relationship with Yoko and the child than to be seen.

YOKO ONO: And I think another thing that we noticed in the sixties when we were waving flags and bags or whatever, you know and . . . all these people were trying to change society for the good and all that, they'd be running around sort of with bags and banners and . . . but at the same time they forget their families and they have a split or, you know, whatever, a divorce, and the children are ignored and wives are resentful and, you know, that sort of thing, so we felt that we had to try to clean up our personal life as well, sort of, like, really take care of each other, you know.

JOHN LENNON: Well, even with the Jerry Rubins and the Tariq Alis and that we'd always comment to them and after they'd left, well, where's the women, you know? Where's the women running *Red Mole*? Where's the women socialists? Where's the women left wingers? Where's the women in on the meeting about how they're going to overthrow the government? Or whatever the hell they were talking about.

YOKO ONO: And Jerry's girlfriend typing his let . . . you know, thesis or something, you know, speech or whatever . . . typical.

JOHN LENNON: They're all going to liberate the world, but they're all doing the typing and making the coffee, you know. Come on, this is garbage but, you know, it took us time to see through it all like that.

ANDY PEEBLES: Can we just go backwards just for a moment?

JOHN LENNON: Sure.

ANDY PEEBLES: Because there are about three things I want to deal with and then we'll come back to the album, and up to date again, I'm sorry about this . . .

JOHN LENNON: Fine.

ANDY PEEBLES: October 1974, we've got to play *Whatever Gets You Through The Night* which I think . . .

JOHN LENNON: . . . oh, Elton, yes . . .

ANDY PEEBLES: Yeah, Elton who I did a programme similar to

62

this with, not so very long ago, and we see quite a lot of in London when he's not worrying about the finances of his football club which he does these days.

JOHN LENNON: Watford, right?

ANDY PEEBLES: Yes, he's doing a good job there. Vocals, piano and organ. Had you known each other a long time, because Elton would appear to have been around the business quite a while when you first met the man!

JOHN LENNON: I didn't meet him until he was big and famous. Let me think, you have got me here, I can't re . . . I met him through Tony King I think, who was a mutual friend who, Tony had worked at Apple but he also worked at Decca and all various places in London, and he was a friend of that great DJ [Tony Hall] who was a friend of George's, God it has gone out of my head now. But he also, he brought the Ronettes over, introduced the Beatles to the Ronettes in his flat in London and he was hip to the Motown stuff very early and all that and you'll – mystery man – he'll know who he is if he's listening. Anyway it was Tony King, I think, and how that record came about was that Elton was in town and I was doing it and needed a harmony, he did the harmony on that and a couple more, and played beautiful piano on it, and jokingly he was telling me he was going to do this Madison Square Garden concert and he said, will you do it with me if the record's Number One? And I did not expect it to get to Number One at all. I didn't think it had a chance in hell, because my, you know, I wasn't being very well received on any level then, you know, with the Kotexes and the hamburgers or, whatever. Well I said, sure, sure I would, sure I will. Well, I lived to get nervous about that, because a year later or whenever it was, he came back and said, okay it's time to pay your dues.

ANDY PEEBLES: And the record went to Number One.

JOHN LENNON: Yeah, and it was the first Number One I had actually. *Imagine* wasn't Number One, *Instant Karma* wasn't Number One which I think were all better records than *Whatever Gets You Through The Night*, words are pretty good, but anyway so what could we sing? That was the point, so we sang Paul's song, *I Saw Her Standing There*. So I'm on

Elton's record, but it was quite nice and that's when Yoko and I got back together the night I performed with Elton at Madison Square Garden. And I went on there and did the number and I was quite astonished that the crowd was so nice to me, because I was only judging by what the papers said about me, and I thought I may as well not be around you know. And the crowd was fantastic.

YOKO ONO: Let me explain that. Because I was in the audience, and Elton came and he performed, and this was the first time I saw Elton perform, and he's just a fantastic performer, you know, the performer of the century – that's the way I felt that night – he was sort of very heavy and very good. And I was watching and everybody was supporting and all that, but when John came out and it was Madison Square Garden and just the whole hall was sort of shaking, because everybody was just jumping and applauding and screaming and shouting . . . an amazing scene, you know, and literally the floor, that floor was shaking. I thought it was like an earthquake, you know. And so John came out like that and because it was a surprise sort of a thing, I suppose, but anyway he was standing there and so everybody, I mean, I'm sure that people thought that this was great, you know. But the John that I observed was a different John, I thought, oh he looks so lonely, you know, he looks so lonely out there.

ANDY PEEBLES: That's my man out there!

YOKO ONO: And I was sort of like . . . feeling choked, you know.

JOHN LENNON: I didn't know she was in the audience . . . I couldn't have gone on if I'd known she was there . . . came off stage and there she was, you know, and we looked at each other. Oh, oh like the Indica Gallery scene again and that's when we got together that night, so that's a happy memory that whole period.

ANDY PEEBLES: Great stuff, yeah. Right. *Number 9 Dream* came up in February 1975 from the album, another much-played track in Great Britain and I daresay here as well.

JOHN LENNON: Yeah, it got to about Number Nine actually, actually that was written by me, I wrote that, that's what I call craftsmanship writing, meaning, you know, I just churned that out. I'm not putting it down, it's just what it is, but I just sat down and wrote it, you know, with no real inspiration based on a dream I'd had. But I thought, I need a track. I wrote it round the string arrangement I'd written for Harry Nilsson's album I'd produced. *Many Rivers To Cross*, the Jimmy Cliff number I'd done this string arrangement for that and it was such a nice melody on the strings. I thought this is a tune, you know, so I just wrote words to the string arrangement, that was *Number 9 Dream*, kind of psychedelic dreamy kind of thing.

ANDY PEEBLES: In March 1975, as we mentioned in an earlier conversation, you teamed up with David Bowie on *Fame*?

JOHN LENNON: Yeah, because those, I was never in the London scene in the Sixties; whereas George and Paul would be going round everybody's sessions all the time, you know, and playing with everybody, I never played anywhere without the Beatles. I never jammed around with people at all.

ANDY PEEBLES: Loyalty, or it just didn't interest you?

JOHN LENNON: No, shyness, insecurity and I couldn't go in a session and play like George plays, you know, a limited vocabulary on the guitar and the piano. So what could I do going in with Cream, or whatever they would do in those days. So we never hung out in the clubs playing, I hung out in the discos boogying and drinking and that, but I never did that bit. Then suddenly I was working with Elton, and Bowie was around, and we were talking and that, and he'd say come down. And I found myself doing that, you know, but he's fiddling round, he writes them in the studio now; he goes in with about four words and a few guys, and starts laying down all this stuff and he has virtually nothing – he's making it up in the studio. So I just contributed, whatever I contributed which is, you know, like backwards piano and 'Ooh' and a couple of things – a repeat of *Fame* and then we needed a middle eight. So we took some Stevie Wonder middle eight and did it backwards, you know, and we made a record out of it, right? So he got his first Number One. I felt like, that was like a karmic thing you know Elton gave, with me and Elton I got my first Number One, so I passed it on to Bowie and he got his first and I like that track.

ANDY PEEBLES: Yes, remarkable.

YOKO ONO: It's a nice track.

JOHN LENNON: Yeah I love it.

ANDY PEEBLES: Clever man. We mentioned *Elephant Man* earlier – which we've been to see while we've been here in New York – I must say a stunning performance from Bowie, he's a very talented gentleman.

JOHN LENNON: Amazing guy isn't he?

ANDY PEEBLES: I mean I was quite puzzled by that, because I thought, I wonder whether David starring in a stage play like that would encourage the wrong sort of people to turn up. The screamers might come to see Bowie and to say, to hell with the intellectual element of the play, we're just here to clock him, and it wasn't like that at all actually, it was a very sympathetic audience.

JOHN LENNON: I must say I admire him for the vast repertoire of talent the guy has, you know. I was never around when the Ziggy Stardust thing came, because I'd already left England while all that was going on, so I never really knew what he was. And meeting him doesn't give you much more of a clue, you know.

ANDY PEEBLES: That's very true, very true.

JOHN LENNON: Because you don't know which one you're talking to. But . . . and, you know, we all have our little personality traits, so between him and me I don't know what was going down but we seemed to have some kind of communication together, and I think he's great. The fact that he can just walk into that and do that I could never do that.

ANDY PEEBLES: You did *Across the Universe* on that album . . .

JOHN LENNON: You could never go and do *Elephant Man.*

YOKO ONO: You can . . .

JOHN LENNON: She's great, she tells me I can do everything. Make a movie, you know, because you only have to learn two lines at once.

YOKO ONO: I'm not talking about specifically *Elephant Man* . . .

JOHN LENNON: I can't even remember my own lyrics, so I couldn't go on stage and remember all that.

ANDY PEEBLES: Do you remember doing *Across the Universe*

with Bowie? You played guitar on that.

JOHN LENNON: Did I play on that too? Oh yeah, my God, jeeze, I did too. I didn't remember that. No, I only remember the *Fame* session.

ANDY PEEBLES: 1975, *The Rock 'n' Roll Album*, which was all oldies, which was a collaboration with Phil Spector, a lot of die-hard fans of the old days in Britain would say, yeah, John Lennon's our King Rocker . . .

JOHN LENNON: Oh, that's nice.

ANDY PEEBLES: How does John Lennon feel about that statement? Three people said that to me before I left London. Friends of mine . . .

JOHN LENNON: Well, good on you, I knight you as the King of Rock, I now call you Sir whoever.

ANDY PEEBLES: You did *Be-Bop-a-Lula*, *Sweet Sixteen*, . . .

JOHN LENNON: Yes, there's millions. I would do albums of that stuff, but I get slagged off 'Oh he can't write any more'. I like to just go . . .

ANDY PEEBLES: Was that the case at the time, John?

JOHN LENNON: There was a bit of that. Oh, he's run dry so he has to do these. I did them for the pure hell of it. And that was the first one where I gave Spector his head, although it came to a different kind of head in the end. That's another long story, if you look at the album there's about five of Spector's, then there's five I knocked off in five days. Which is *Be-Bop-a-Lula*. The Holly stuff and the Carla Thomas, Sam Cooke's all that, because he ran away with the tapes. He called me . . . Yeah, he ran off with the sixteen tracks and locked them in his garage or somewhere I couldn't get them. Then he called me one night. A very far out guy, now he calls me and says . . .

YOKO ONO: And we are in the middle of the session.

JOHN LENNON: . . . but . . . because they had never got that close to him on the *Imagine* and the Plastic Ono thing, because he'd been very good and just come and gone away again, and I hadn't really got to know him. On the *Rock 'n' Roll* it took me three weeks to convince him that I wasn't going to co-produce with him, and I wasn't going to go in the control room, I was only . . . I said I just want to be the singer, just treat me like

Ronnie [Spector]. We'll pick the material, I just want to sing, I don't want anything to do with production or writing or creation, I just want to sing. So I finally convinced him, anyway – long story short. One day when he didn't want to work, one night he called me, he said the studio has been burnt down. Now these . . . in the early days I didn't know about it, you know, didn't know how far away he was. So I said, Oh the studio's burnt down. So anyway a couple of hours passed . . . the studio's burnt down . . . So I get somebody to call the studio, it hadn't been burnt down. That was the Sunday, the following Sunday he calls and he says on the phone, 'Hey Johnny' . . . I said, Oh there you are, Phil, what happened? We're supposed to be doing a session. 'I got the John Dean tapes.' I says, what? 'I got the John Dean tapes.'

ANDY PEEBLES: Watergate!

JOHN LENNON: Right, Watergate. I said, what are you do . . . what are you talking about? He said, 'The house is surrounded by helicopters now, they are trying to get them.' I said, the house is surrounded? I'm buying this garbage . . . I'm saying the house is surrounded, you've got the John Dean tapes. I said, well what about our session? Aren't we supposed to be finishing, or something, you know, it's costing money. And he . . . I said what are you doing with the John . . .? He said, 'I'm the only one that knows how to tell whether they've been doctored or edited or not.' What he was telling me, in his own sweet way, was he had my tapes, not the John Dean Watergate tapes, he had my tapes locked in the cellar behind the barbed wire and the Afghan dogs and the machine guns. So there was no way you could get them. So that album was stopped in the middle for a year, and we had to sue through Capitol to get them back off him. By then it had been going on and on and on and it was the Tampax lost weekend period as well, and it was all hell was going on . . . And I'd somehow got committed to producing Harry Nilsson's album which . . . that's when I sobered up in Harry Nilsson's album, because I took Keith Moon and Harry and all them, and I'd lost the John Dean tapes, I'd lost them so that album was quick. I'd promised Harry in a drunken stupor I'd produce him, and I suddenly, and we rented this house, I thought get them all in one house and they'll behave themselves. So we'd got Keith Moon . . .

YOKO ONO: Which was not true.

JOHN LENNON: It was the wrong thing to do. I'd Keith Moon, Harry Nillson and Ringo . . . all these people living in a house on the beach, where formerly Kennedy and Marilyn had been, or something like that, on one of those LA houses on the beach. And one day I realised, Jesus I'm the producer, they are going to be asking me where the tapes are. You know? And we'd go in, the bottle would be out and everybody was just falling on the floor and nobody was working, so I sobered up then, I just quit, cold turkey, the drink. Finished off Harry's album. Harry doesn't know when to quit. He wants to go on and on and on mixing, every time he mixed it, he wants to do it again. So I ran away to New York with the Harry tapes. I didn't steal them. I said, Harry, you've got to leave me alone to finish this, I'm supposed to be producing it. He followed me to New York. I finally had to turn round and say, Harry, get the hell out, I want to finish this record. And then suddenly they sent me the . . . We got the *Rock 'n' Roll* tapes back from Spector, finally, and I was in the middle of *Walls and Bridges*, and all hell was going on and I finished off the Rock and Roll thing in five days. I did about eight tracks all in – one after the other – because what I found is I just sort of relaxed. All the words to *Stand by Me*, *Be-Bop-a-Lula* I knew them all from being fifteen, they all just came back just like that. So it was simple. So I did that. But funnily enough, at the end of the *Rock 'n' Roll* and on a track called *Just Because*, which Phil wanted me to sing – I didn't know it that well, you hear me saying, 'And so we say farewell from Record Plant West' . . . And something flashed through me mind as I said it, am I really saying farewell to the business? It wasn't conscious and it was a long, long time before I did take time out. And I looked at the cover which I'd chosen which was a picture of me in Hamburg the first time we got there.

ANDY PEEBLES: That's right.

JOHN LENNON: And I thought is this, am I going . . .? And the other famous picture that's around in all the Beatle books is a picture of me on stage with the group before Paul had joined, and I'm in a white jacket. It's in the Hunter Davis book and all of them. That was the day, the first day I sang *Be-Bop-a-Lula* at a church fête with a band called The Quarrymen. It was the day I met Paul and he was in the audience, a mutual friend had brought him. I thought is this some sort of comic thing, here I am with this old picture of me in Hamburg in '61, and I'm saying farewell from Record Plant, and I'm ending as I started, singing this straight Rock 'n' Roll stuff.

ANDY PEEBLES: Very interesting analogy.

JOHN LENNON: I'd had no conscious . . . It was only years later when I looked back and thinking was I saying that? Because that was really the last record I made, even though it came out at a different order from *Walls and Bridges* and I think. They came out backwards order, because of what Phil had done with the 'John Dean tapes'!

ANDY PEEBLES: Interesting story.

JOHN LENNON: 'Helicopters all round the building, John . . .'

ANDY PEEBLES: Then there was the *Shaved Fish* album which was a collection of hit singles.

JOHN LENNON: Well, hits and misses, I think, and nears. Well, when I realised . . . That was another thing – was it a subconscious move? Did I know I wasn't going to be on Capitol and EMI any more? I had no intentions, no thoughts about it. But what I found out was, when I went to look for the *Cold Turkey* master tapes, nobody knew where they were, I had to use dubs of *Power to the People* because the tapes had gone, nobody could give a damn at the record companies because they weren't . . . you know, that big. Big enough for them to be interested. So what I realised was if I don't put this *Shaved Fish* thing together, that's why I didn't call it oldies or goldies or the Best of, because it wasn't – some of them didn't hardly get any air play. But I thought if I don't put this package together, some of the works is just going to go . . . nobody's . . . they will be lost for ever. So I've put it together and sort of . . . at least it's there now for anybody whose interested.

ANDY PEEBLES: On that subject, are you aware of the amount of Beatles product that has been reissued in various forms over the last few years? We've had an album of the Beatles Ballads, we've had the Beatles doing Rock 'n' Roll. We've almost had the Beatles doing things the Beatles didn't do.

JOHN LENNON: I know, some of them I was aware of, because they would call about it and I asked for George Martin to reproduce them, they wanted to do them in some way . . . that double package that they did. And I was involved in that respect – just checking the condition of them, because I didn't want lousy versions going out, I wanted them to be as was. And I asked Capitol/EMI, or EMI/Capitol whichever, please ask George Martin would he take care of this, so at least he knows what to do. I didn't want some strange guy, you know, making dubbed versions of it and putting it out, because of the versions that were going out, the reissues were pretty poor. I hadn't even listened to them, because I just presumed they'd take the tape as we made it and make a master and put it out again, but they didn't, they'd been screwing around with a few of the early ones. I didn't know that until it was too late. So on that last package where they had Beatles 60 . . . different periods – that one. I made sure . . .

ANDY PEEBLES: *The Red* and *The Blue*?

JOHN LENNON: *The Red* and *The Blue* that one. I made sure George Martin was there and I made sure they put that picture which I got Linda to take of the same pose as their very first album over the Abbey Road . . . No what is it that . . . EMI office in some other place, some square?

ANDY PEEBLES: Manchester Square.

JOHN LENNON: Manchester Square. So I was involved in that respect, in that package making sure that the cover was what I wanted and that the sound was done by George Martin. So I don't mind that one.

YOKO ONO: And you checked the remixes too . . .

JOHN LENNON: Checked the remix after he'd done it, it was as good as you could get out of whatever mono recording we did then.

ANDY PEEBLES: Vocals right, everything else left, or vice versa.

JOHN LENNON: Yes that surprised me, I don't know what we were doing there. I want to talk to George Martin, why were we always putting the drums on the right and why wasn't it in the middle? I was surprised. I always thought in terms of mono anyway, I wasn't that sold on stereo.

ANDY PEEBLES: Almost made Kenny Everett an extra Beatle you know . . . some wonderful editing jobs.

JOHN LENNON: Well, Jack Douglas who worked with us on this thing *Double Fantasy* and he worked with us on *Fly* and *Mind Games*, he goes way back. He was the young engineer in those days. Well, he was saying the way they learnt how to reproduce Beatle music in studios and on stage was because of those extraordinary stereo things. They could isolate the vocals, the harmony and learn that, and then isolate the other side and learn that, and that's what they were doing. I don't know why the hell we did that. I'll have to ask George Martin because a lot of it was done before I knew what, the recording studio was really a big tape recorder, then it was like a space ship, rather like a space ship to me.

ANDY PEEBLES: 1975, when you retired and went underground for want of a better phrase, you said 'I have made my contribution to society . . .'

JOHN LENNON: I didn't . . .

YOKO ONO: No . . .

JOHN LENNON: This is the funny thing. You know how you were saying, well, were you laughing during the Bed-in's and the Bag-in's and all that? It's funny that you are laughing about it, of course we were laughing, we had fun. Also the fun of when we weren't doing anything was all these amazing stories. They had in the *Daily Mail*, *Daily Express* that I'd gone bald, that was . . . they showed before and after pictures, you know, they used a picture of me with a beret on.

ANDY PEEBLES: You shouldn't have played with Elton John!

JOHN LENNON: So anyway a couple of stories went round, one that I'd gone completely bald and the other was that I'd made this extraordinary statement. I mean I don't even hear how I talk, can you imagine me saying that. I've made my contribution to society . . . what was it . . .?

ANDY PEEBLES: That was pretty well . . .

JOHN LENNON: And I'll no longer work again, I think was the

whole quote. I never said that, because I didn't talk to any reporters or radio people.

YOKO ONO: Or anybody.

JOHN LENNON: Or anybody for the five years that I was underground as you call it. I didn't talk to anybody so I never said it, I don't know where they got it from.

YOKO ONO: And we were way overground on the seventh floor . . .

JOHN LENNON: We were high as kites my dear . . . underground. That was the news media . . . You see how the media self perpetuates itself. Now the first interview we did after the five years, we chose to do through *Newsweek*, for whatever reasons.

ANDY PEEBLES: I've read it.

JOHN LENNON: Right, Okay, so they ask us the questions. She goes back, the editor puts . . . rephrases the questions and when she sat down with me with a little tape recorder and said, what were you doing? What made you withdraw from the public for five years? . . . was how she put it. When she gets back the editor says, underground. You know why? I've worked out the psychology because Abbie Hoffman had just come out from the underground so they tie Hoffman, Lennon, Oh why were you underground? I wasn't underground. I was overground. I was all over the place like I said, all over the world travelling, and we were doing all kinds of business, you might have heard cows and all that sort of stuff. I mean we were pretty damn active, we just weren't in the papers, we weren't available for comment, that's all.

ANDY PEEBLES: Did you say something to the extent that life doesn't end when you cut off your subscription to *Billboard*!

JOHN LENNON: Right. Because I literally cut off. I did say that, but I said that after. The quotes are correct in *Newsweek*, it's just that the questions were rephrased. So lets not perpetuate the underground, there's no underground about it, we were not underground at all.

YOKO ONO: We had a good time.

JOHN LENNON: We were having a fine, fine old time, it's just that we weren't . . . we were making no comment, when Elvis died people were harassing me in Tokyo for a comment. Well I'll give it you now: he died when he went into the Army. You know, that's when they killed him, that's when they castrated him, the rest of it was just a living death.

ANDY PEEBLES: You said that you reversed roles . . . that John . . .

YOKO ONO: Yes, my dear . . .?

ANDY PEEBLES: Looked after Sean. How good a cook are you, John?

JOHN LENNON: Not bad, not great. I've mastered the art of rice, they say anyone can cook rice but few people cook it well. I can cook it reasonably well. I can do fish.

YOKO ONO: You're a good bread maker.

JOHN LENNON: I've learned to make bread which I was thrilled with, I took a Polaroid of me first bread, you know. These two . . . I couldn't believe they came out like that.

YOKO ONO: In a good old macho tradition, he had to record it in history.

JOHN LENNON: I was thrilled, it's not macho anybody . . . it was the first bread. It looked great, you know, and it tasted good, that was pretty damned good, and so for about half a year, or a year, I was providing the food for the . . . for Yoko, the baby, even the staff was eating. I was so excited that I could do it, that I would stop, bring all the staff in to each lunch, you know. But after a bit it was wearing me out. Because life becomes as most housewives know . . .

YOKO ONO: A routine.

JOHN LENNON: A routine between the meals, you see. So people were saying, well weren't you thinking about this, that and the other? You don't, because you think from breakfast, once the baby's had the breakfast, they've had their breakfast you've got about an hour . . . you know before breakfast starts you've got a little time to yourself for coffee and a smoke or whatever, and then everybody comes up, wants to eat. Okay feed them, you don't get a gold record, they just swallow it, you know. If they swallow it, that means you were a hit, if they don't swallow it, that means you did something wrong . . .

YOKO ONO: But that's what most women go through . . .

74

JOHN LENNON: Yeah, that's how I really feminised in a different way, and it was quite an experience, the equivalent to say going to a monastery and withdrawing in that way, but not withdrawing to . . . going to a Zen monastery and going to India to meditate or going to Scotland and growing, talking to bananas, you know, melons or something. Whatever they are doing up there in that place, the famous place that's supposed to grow big veg or something. So, in that way, it was withdrawal by becoming, it was a Zen experience to master that cooking thing and put as much energy into that bread . . . and make it right . . .

YOKO ONO: Which disappears very quickly.

JOHN LENNON: Not just whack it away . . . I took it from scratch. Now I buy a packet of Pilsbury or something, it blows up into bread. From scratch with the flour and the hand, doing by hand. And then the time between breakfast and lunch is very quick, you hardly had time to read the paper, that's presuming it ain't raining and the babysitter can take the child out, so you get a break from the constant Daddy, look at this; Daddy, look at that, you know, look at me, look at me . . . feed the cat. Then it's bloody lunchtime. So this went on for about nine months, I really enjoyed it, you know, because I concentrated, I put me mind to it. But it's the meals, the meals is what you live, you live the regulation of between meals. And on the other side of me there's always just being served by women, whether it was my Auntie Mimi, God Bless You! And or whoever – served by females, wives, girlfriends. You just sort of flop in drunk and expect some girlfriend at college to make the breakfast the next morning, you know she'd been drunk as a dog too, with you at the party, female is supposed suddenly to get on the other side of the counter. It was quite an experience, and I appreciated what women have done for me all my life. I'd never even thought about it.

YOKO ONO: A woman's work is never done, you know . . .

JOHN LENNON: It's so true, love, you're never ever done.

YOKO ONO: And, you know, he makes the bread . . . and if you make bread, you know, you want people to eat it, you know, and if they don't eat it it's a personal insult. So we went through that one. Oh Yoko, aren't you eating this? I made it . . .

JOHN LENNON: Ah, you didn't like the bread yesterday.

YOKO ONO: No, it's just that I'm not hungry . . . you know.

JOHN LENNON: Well, you know, mother's always hanging round saying, eat up, clean up your plate, because you've put all the sweat into it, and then the kid comes in, I don't like sausage . . .

ANDY PEEBLES: Did you become a dictatorial mother and did you not appreciate . . .?

YOKO ONO: No he wasn't, but he was going through the experience in a sort of tongue in cheek way, and . . .

JOHN LENNON: They loved the bread, I'd make you two on Fridays, supposed to last a week, it'd be gone Saturday afternoon, you know – whoom. Like pigs – whomph it'd gone, so I started buying the bread again. Pretty damned quick.

YOKO ONO: Well, if we don't eat it you are offended, if we eat it up, you think well then I have to make it again.

JOHN LENNON: But I enjoyed it, and I looked on it as a discipline, an absolute discipline, and that's how I approached it. Through that I got into a whole other new world.

ANDY PEEBLES: And one of the most important facets of that world surely was it gave you a great deal of time to spend with your son, Sean.

JOHN LENNON: Yes, because between Yoko and I – I cannot do figures and numbers, I'm not good at business, and somebody has to take the business, care of business, whether it was Beatle, Apples or surviving inflation or whatever you call it. And there's no way I can do it. I don't have that talent. So she had to do it. She has the talent to do it. And so I had to contribute something, not just sit around either talking about the former greatness of the Beatles or the fact that when I'm not writing songs, so what am I supposed to do? So I had the sort of sibling, or the early relationship with Sean, because she would go to the office even though the office was only downstairs in the same building, she was still not there. And so Sean and I would spend this time together. And it was fantastic because as I said in an interview, with Julian my first child, I would come home and there'd be a twelve-year-old-boy there who I had no

relationship with whatsoever. Now he's seventeen, I'm getting
a relationship now because I can talk and . . . about music and
whatever he's got into and girlfriends and that kind of stuff . . .
I'd come back from Australia and he'd be a different size,
I wouldn't even recognise how he looked, half the time. And
the timing was just right for me to do all that, as well. And it's
great the jokes, they did a thing on *Saturday Night Live*
[American TV programme], you know they had me in an
apron and Yoko with the tie and all that, and they did a real
good skit on us and we were hysterical, you know, I mean it
was just very, very funny. All the time I kept saying, Oh look
the oven's burning . . . and that was the skit of me. I don't mind
the mickey taking at all, because to me I approached it
intellectually. First as a kind of Zen discipline, make the bed,
conquered the rice, conquered that dependence on woman,
even if I'm alone, I can now cook . . . enough to get by.
YOKO ONO: I mean most men probably resent the fact that
they have to depend on women – all those things – you know.
ANDY PEEBLES: They like their independence, they like to be
able to go in the kitchen and cook.
JOHN LENNON: When I think about it, at school I wish they'd
taught us practical things. I wish I'd been taught to type, so I
could write quickly, which I've self-taught meself but it's
still not fast enough. I wish I'd been taught to cook so I could
look after meself when my Auntie was not there or something . . .
or whenever, when I was a bit older and coming in at odd times,
or living in a flat when I was at college. Suddenly there's this
tin of beans, you know, or living on fish and chips, and if you
were just taught to cook, type and a few practical things, to
drive, instead of all this garbage about . . . whatever the
teachers were trying to teach us at school . . . the spinning
jenny and all . . . I don't give a damn about the spinning jenny.
YOKO ONO: What's that?
JOHN LENNON: Some invention . . . 1492 Columbus sailed . . . yes.
ANDY PEEBLES: Well, as I sit here talking to you, you look two
very happy people. Which of you, or was it both of you, who
first got in contact with David Geffen? Presuming that you make
the contacts.

JOHN LENNON: He made the contacts.

YOKO ONO: Yes, he did first.

JOHN LENNON: She did the deal.

YOKO ONO: And then I just called him back.

ANDY PEEBLES: And from that telephone call or whatever it was . . .

YOKO ONO: And we decided to meet and so he came to my office. Oh yes, he came to my office and, sort of, I was checking him, you know, he was all right.

JOHN LENNON: You see, the point about me cooking and her doing the business, before we'd always had somebody come in to look after the business and, you know the story of that, it's all . . .

ANDY PEEBLES: History.

JOHN LENNON: Some lawyer or some accountant would come in and say I'll handle it all for you. Since 1962 they've been handling it, and then nothing but tax problems and, you know, whatever. For a long history of it. Like we don't own any of the Beatles songs, we don't own any of the Beatle records, we've got farthings for royalties and all the rest of it. Anyway, the point being, we decided not to have an outside party. We had to look after our own stuff and face that reality. She could deal with it, so I could go to the other side which I could deal with. I'm a homebody, I always like to hang around the house.

YOKO ONO: I'm sure there are many men who feel that way. About the fact that they really would like to be at home, see to the baby, or maybe just cooking. A lot of men are very good cooks, you know, and they like to exercise that talent but then it's supposed to be something sissy and something you are not supposed to do. There's that. And also it's mentally healthy to sort of exchange roles, to see the other side and that sort of thing.

ANDY PEEBLES: So along came this offer, and you made the decision to record the album, *Double Fantasy* which we've been hearing a lot of recently. You also told me, John, that there were what? Twenty-two tracks originally, you'd included fourteen and a little while ago I was hearing something which isn't on the album which is very interesting indeed.

JOHN LENNON: Yes, we . . . actually we recorded the album before we talked together.

YOKO ONO: Right. Exactly.

JOHN LENNON: We decided to have made it first and answer all the letters and enquiries that came, you know, wanting to have the album, you know, we eliminated the ones that says, can we hear it first? Okay, you can go to hell, you know, forget about him, you know . . . if you don't trust . . .

YOKO ONO: Who the hell to say . . .

JOHN LENNON: If you can't trust, after all those years, forget it. I don't want to know about it. Also he wasn't a big company, so you weren't dealing with this anonymous grey suit, you know, with the president changing every two days, there was always more presidents of Capitol than EMI, they were always waiting for the Beatles to die, they died first every time. They always treated each record as the last record.

ANDY PEEBLES: In this stage of negotiation, did the old fear come back from the old days, that you were having to take a step which involved somebody else?

JOHN LENNON: It did, yes I was terrified. I was saying can we put it out without, without putting it out? Couldn't we do something else? Do I have to put me name on the paper? Because I've only, you know, for the last five years . . . the first time I didn't owe somebody songs or records for the last fifteen or twenty years. Since 1962 I was signed up to somebody or other, and thankful to be in 1962, but what you sign when you are twenty-one and it goes on for twenty years and they all own you, life and soul and you can never get out of it. So I liked the five years when all contracts were free. I was free of any contractual obligation when she finally says, look you are going to have to sign something to say that they have the right to put the record out. I was saying you're sure? You're sure? Why don't you sign it? You figure it, I don't want to put me name on it, but we made arrangements which didn't make me feel paranoid because I don't want to owe people nothing. I don't want to . . . the point of being a musician or artist to me was the freedom.

ANDY PEEBLES: How easy was it to get musicians together?

JOHN LENNON: Oh easy, they were panting at the doors, they all couldn't wait to get in. All the ones I used to work with were sending messages. I felt bad but I didn't want to go back in the same bag, you know. I heard from Jesse Davies and Klaus and all of them but I didn't . . . I wanted to start really brand new.

YOKO ONO: You were very lucky.

JOHN LENNON: The only guy I knew was Hugh McCracken who'd worked on the Christmas song – the one you mentioned and maybe a couple more tracks.

ANDY PEEBLES: And you got Andy Newmark on drums.

JOHN LENNON: Yeah, who'd toured with George.

ANDY PEEBLES: Somebody you'd known for a fair while, I presume?

JOHN LENNON: No, no, I might have met him backstage when George did some concert tour, not in New York, across the water, I never remember, New Jersey or somewhere, and I probably met him backstage. I don't remember him at all. And Tony Levine the bass player, fantastic . . . I didn't even know he existed, he was famous but I didn't know he'd worked with all sorts of people. So, no, the only guy I knew was Hugh McCracken, I'd used him as a New York guy. Earl Slick who was Bowie's R . . . when Bowie was in his R & B incarnation that period – mid-seventies – Earl Slick had been his guitarist but I hadn't met him, even though he was on the *Fame* album, we were not in the studio at the same time.

ANDY PEEBLES: And you recorded it where we're sat at this very moment at the Hit Factory.

JOHN LENNON: 'Yes, this is the very room, the very room where it happened.' You know the Double Fantasy was brought alive, as it were, in this very bloody room, wasn't it, dear?

YOKO ONO: Yes.

ANDY PEEBLES: You're wasted, Mr Lennon, you're wasted!

JOHN LENNON: I love *Fawlty Towers*, I'd like to be in that. You know part of me would sooner have been a comedian, you know. I just don't have the guts to stand up and do it but I'd love to be in Monty Python, you know, rather than the Beatles.

YOKO ONO: That's the thing that saved us, you know, the fact that he's funny, you know, and he says I'm funny so, you know, we both make each other laugh in a way, you know.

JOHN LENNON: *Fawlty Towers* is the greatest show I've seen in years. They have it over here now. God, it's great I mean, what a guy, he's great. I saw him explaining how he only gets half an hour to do it and produce it once a week but what a masterpiece, a beautiful thing.

ANDY PEEBLES: We now have a new one called *Not the Nine O'clock News* which runs on a Monday night while the Nine O'clock News is running on BBC One.

YOKO ONO: Oh, great.

JOHN LENNON: Well, it'll come over here. Public TV here buys them all you see. We get all the Masterpiece series stuff. We cried our way through, what is it, *Lydia*, oh everything, all those series, watch them all. Beautiful stuff you know. I see all the English countryside then I think, oh well, it saves getting on the plane and there it is all green and wet and it looks beautiful even though I'm here. It's . . . the voyeurism, it's being in England without being there.

ANDY PEEBLES: Let's talk about the single *Just Like Starting Over*. Was that an obvious choice for the both of you, as a single? Were you happy with that?

JOHN LENNON: Yeah, because it was . . .

YOKO ONO: It's the message.

JOHN LENNON: It was really called *Starting Over* but, while we're making it, people kept putting things out with the same title. You know, there was a country and western hit called *Starting Over*, so I added 'Just Like' at the last minute. The thing was, it was obvious because it was the one where the musicians got very loose because it was so simple rock 'n' roll, there was no problem. They really relaxed and they'd all be like that after it. And it just, even though I don't think it's the strongest track perhaps but it was in . . . some of the other tracks are stronger, I mean *Like Losing You* might be a stronger piece of material, but *Starting Over* was the best way to start over. And to me it was like going back to fifteen and singing à la Presley. All the time I was referring to John [Smith], the engineer, here in the room I was referring to Elvis Orbison. It's kinda *I Want You, I need . . . Only The Lonely*, you know . . .

(*Sings*) . . . a kind of parody but not really parody.

ANDY PEEBLES: A little tongue in cheek?

YOKO ONO: Oh very.

JOHN LENNON: A little! . . . Oh when I was doing it, I was cracking up . . . (*Sings*) . . .

ANDY PEEBLES: You relieve me greatly, because we still do *Round Table*, the review show on Radio One, and I was one of the guests the night that the Lennon single arrived in the studio, and there was absolute panic and pandemonium and it was on the turntable and the man who hosts the show, Adrian Love, said to me, what do you think? And I said, terrific but a little tongue in cheek.

JOHN LENNON: Right exactly . . . some people took it seriously, you know, saying what's he trying to do and all that but, you know, they forget . . .

YOKO ONO: They, he was winking, you know, that one.

JOHN LENNON: I've had tongue in cheek all along. *I'm the Walrus*, all of them had tongue in cheek, you know, I don't, just because other people see depths of whatever in it, you know, what does it really mean 'I Am the Eggman'? You know, it could have been the pudding basin for all I cared. It was just tongue in cheek, it's not that serious.

ANDY PEEBLES: Do you, and did you, get fed up with people ostracising your lyrics and trying to read marvellously intellectual interpretations into them? Both of you, this must apply to?

JOHN LENNON: It was fun, sometimes it's fun but then it gets to be stupid, you know, that's why I started from the *Mother* album onwards trying to shave off all imagery, pretensions of poetry, illusions of grandeur, I call à la Dylan Dylanesque, you know. I didn't write any of that. Just say what it is, simple English, make it rhyme and put a backbeat on it and express yourself as simply as possible, straightforwardly as possible. As they say, Northern people are blunt, right, so I was trying to write like I am and I enjoy the poetic side and I'll probably do a little dabble later because Yoko's lyrics are so poetic. I get, well maybe I should do some of that, you know, and the track you were talking about *Walking on Thin Ice* was one of the extra tracks. We cut twenty-two tracks in ten days, I mean we were just like had diarrhoea of rock here, you know, and we just zapped out these twenty-two tracks and got it down to fourteen; and one I played you before was *Walking on Thin Ice* which was one of Yoko's tracks that we didn't put on for many, many reasons. Some were selected, some not.

ANDY PEEBLES: Which is a marvellous dance track, I must hastily add.

JOHN LENNON: Well, then *Kiss Kiss Kiss* which is the other side of *Starting Over* is getting a lot of rock club, new wave whatever you call it, disco exposure. So we made a special kind of disc for them, and Yoko came up with the idea why don't we give them something they don't have, and we made a kind of discoesque long six-minute version of *Walking on Thin Ice* which will go out. There's a separate market disco or rock club and it'll go out to them.

YOKO ONO: And we throw in *Open Your Box* which is one that was banned, you know.

JOHN LENNON: Yes, so we've thrown in *Open Your Box* for old time's sake.

ANDY PEEBLES: Tell me about *Kiss Kiss Kiss*, Yoko?

YOKO ONO: What about?

ANDY PEEBLES: About the song.

JOHN LENNON: Tell them how you recorded it in the pitch dark hidden behind these big walls here.

YOKO ONO: Yes, really with *Kiss Kiss Kiss* when recording time . . . I started to do it and then I suddenly looked and all these engineers were all looking, and I thought, I can't do that, you know. So I said, well turn off all the lights and put the screen and so that they put the screen around me and I did it that way.

JOHN LENNON: We were all sitting there saying, what's she doing? She was having an orgasm and nobody was there and I was saying, well . . .

YOKO ONO: It's called acting, you know.

JOHN LENNON: Oh, very good, dear, very good yes, Ziggy Stardust!

ANDY PEEBLES: Do you get embarrassed in the studio, Yoko?

Doing something like that? Do you want to be on your own and a bit shy?

JOHN LENNON: Sorry to interrupt, but there was John, me and Jack and Lee the engineer and a few people we were all in there . . .

YOKO ONO: I'm glad I didn't know that.

JOHN LENNON: She's trying to do, you know, what was it . . . I got the image of that Japanese movie running through the glass, you know.

YOKO ONO: It's a bit like that, isn't it?

JOHN LENNON: You'd better answer the question.

YOKO ONO: Oh well, I mean, I don't understand your question, I mean *Kiss Kiss Kiss* is what it is and the song itself will explain, and so, if you listen to it, you know, you will get all whatever you want to get out of it probably. But it's probably mainly sort of like a feminine and Asian vulnerability that women are not . . . getting scared of exposing now, you know, and it's all right to show vulnerability and in a way it's saying, well, this is woman, you know.

JOHN LENNON: But she was a bit shy and she put up a big screen and put the lights out and we all just heard this sound running through.

ANDY PEEBLES: From what you've just said, the most interesting statement to me is that you, the person listening, would derive what they wish out of it. Do you deliberately produce songs like that? Because it's rather like the movie business, isn't it? You can go and see an adaptation of something and it sticks in your mind as being the adaptation you might remember for the whole of your life. If you write a song and people can derive what they want from it, it's a very personal thing, isn't it? And that's a special way of communicating.

YOKO ONO: Oh yes, well, I think that most of my songs, well, I can't help doing, so I'm not saying I do it intentionally, but it's sort of, I have these visions, visual things, you know, and that comes out. So that it's a visual almost, you know. You can interpret a vision in any way you like, in a way.

ANDY PEEBLES: Do you feel now at this stage, here we are in

December 1980, that the theme and the ease of writing is now back with you?

JOHN LENNON: Yes.

ANDY PEEBLES: And that you're going to be extremely prolific in the months and years to come?

JOHN LENNON: Yes, I think it's going to be the one period they say, Those two will do anything for publicity, for Christ's sake get them off the front pages, oh get them off. You know, people are bitching at us, because we were always doing something; and then they were bitching at us because we weren't doing anything. And I have a funny feeling that it's going to be the other way round again, because we're talking and talking and talking and all sorts of plans and ideas we have in our heads, it's just a matter of getting it done, you know? We already got half the next album, and we'll probably go in just after Christmas and do that. And we're already talking about, what the ideas for the third album is, already laid out and I can't wait, you know. So it's a matter of just getting it done, and I'm sorry about you people that get fed up of hearing about us, but you know, we like to do it, so it's too bad.

ANDY PEEBLES: The problem is, of course, there's always the time gap between you finishing the recording, and people like myself being allowed to sit and talk to you. And that always worries me somewhat, because it's past history to you as you've just said a moment ago, you're two albums ahead of me, as we sit here now.

JOHN LENNON: Right. We're already on the third in our minds, but the second physically, as it were . . . beginning to think about it. But you can't do it at the same time, you see. You can't be discussing it while you're making it. Or you don't even know what you're doing. You're kind of making it and you're so into . . . you cannot be objective about it. I couldn't . . . even some of the records I made, when you talk about them, I don't really, at the time I wasn't consciously knowing what you're doing, in a way. And it's only when you look back at it, you . . . oh, I see what I was feeling at that time, even though one tries to express it in the music, you're not conscious of what you're expressing; and it's sometimes about two or three years later when I've realised what we made then. But *Double Fantasy* I can talk all night about it, but it'll be two years before I can see it really, what it is. How can we talk to you and make it at the same time? It's impossible. It's like inviting you to the rehearsal of a play, you know, and then . . .

ANDY PEEBLES: Changing it the night afterwards?

JOHN LENNON: Right. Even the opening night it can change, the night after, right? So you can't. It's too bad. Too bad.

YOKO ONO: . . . You do need, though, tremendous luck. Tremendous amount of luck . . . probably made us finish that album in a way. I mean the fact that it's man, woman, you know, and the fact that we were able to work together, the fact that the songs came to us at the same time almost, you know as a dialogue, etc, these are just pure luck in a way. It's been given to us almost, hasn't it?

JOHN LENNON: Yeah . . . yeah, and the fact that we can work together and express it in many different ways from starting out with the *Kiss Kiss Kiss.* I mean, the difference is obvious in the sound and everything but we can both be part of both.

ANDY PEEBLES: *Beautiful Boy*, John, a song about Sean?

JOHN LENNON: Yeah. Well, you know, Stevie Wonder wrote about his kid, didn't he? *Isn't He Lovely?*

ANDY PEEBLES: That was recorded here, wasn't it? He did *Songs For In The Key of Life* in this studio, I think I'm right in saying.

JOHN LENNON: Yes, yeah. In Hit Factory, New York, New York. Yeah. Down in, very near Times Square, folks. You come out of here after a session and there's strange women standing on the street. You know, I mean, it's really cooking, it never stops.

ANDY PEEBLES: Yeah.

JOHN LENNON: And, eh, yeah, so at first, funnily enough . . . for the first time I was with Sean in the kitchen with the bread and you know, all that . . . I kept thinking, Well, I ought to be inspired to write about Sean. I mean I ought to. I was going through a bit of that, and when I finally gave up on thinking about writing a song about him, of course, the song came to me. When he was four, four and a half, or five, it was just coming up to October when I suddenly got the song about him.

ANDY PEEBLES: Is he developing an interest in music?

JOHN LENNON: Oh, he's very musical. Absolutely. Because I noticed something in the hospital. This is . . . maybe you don't need this . . . but . . . when the black nurses come in they put on WBLS which is an R & B disco station. When the white nurses would come in, they put on the Country & Western station. When the black nurses fed the babies they picked them up and held them on their hip and danced round the room, and the bottle. When the white nurses came in, they just sit still and jam the bottle down his throat and not move. So I thought, Ahh . . . ha, I want him to have natural rhythm, you know. I mean, . . . seriously, I noticed the different attitude . . . not only was it warmer, and more contact. There was constant movement and officially they weren't allowed to put the radio on. It was not . . . but when the head nurse's away they put it on all the time, because it . . . people don't want their children not being able to sleep without music. Long story short, which I didn't, I did the same with Sean till he could walk. Whenever I fed him, I put the rock and roll on or the R & B and I danced with him. He can dance like nothing on earth. He's perfect pitch in key. He's into *Hound Dog* now, because I said that in an interview, so he thinks it's about hunting. And *Bee-Bop-A-Lula*, he knows backwards.

ANDY PEEBLES: Frankie Crocker is good for your kid? WBLS will love you for that. [Frankie Crocker is the Programme Controller of the WBLS Radio Station].

JOHN LENNON: WBLS . . . (*intoned like the station call-sign*)

ANDY PEEBLES: *Beautiful Boy* is written by John and *Beautiful Boys* is written by Yoko.

YOKO ONO: Yes.

ANDY PEEBLES: One letter?

JOHN LENNON: One letter . . .

YOKO ONO: I just wanted to be creative, you know . . . unique, you know, so I put 's' on.

JOHN LENNON: Oh she's singing about boys and men, right?

YOKO ONO: Mmm, yes, well what about it? . . . Mmm, of course it's a message to John and Sean and all men . . . mmm and eh well, I think, the lyrics will speak for itself, in a way.

ANDY PEEBLES: I'm very pleased that you've actually put your lyrics on the inner sleeve, because one of my major moans in the business, over the last few years, has been that the amount of information available on album sleeves has deteriorated in some cases to absolutely nothing.

JOHN LENNON: You mean they've stopped printing the lyrics?

ANDY PEEBLES: Oh yes, oh yes. And they've stopped telling you who's playing on the album. They've pretty well stopped telling you everything. I wouldn't say that for all record companies but certainly far too many.

JOHN LENNON: It must be financial, right?

ANDY PEEBLES: It could be.

JOHN LENNON: I mean what other reason? They just don't want to spend the money on the print. You know, I'd sooner have the lyrics and no cover.

ANDY PEEBLES: Mmm.

YOKO ONO: It's not much money, I don't think . . . print.

JOHN LENNON: Oh, it is. Every penny counts, love.

YOKO ONO: I know.

ANDY PEEBLES: John, can we talk about *I'm Losing You* which I think reflected your times alone in Hong Kong. Is that when you . . .

JOHN LENNON: Yeah . . .

ANDY PEEBLES: . . . wrote that song?

JOHN LENNON: Well, it wasn't Hong Kong so much as . . . it was actually in Bermuda. I called her, you know, and I couldn't get through. Can you imagine it? . . . she was so busy . . .

YOKO ONO: I was so busy . . .

JOHN LENNON: She was so busy with so many calls that I couldn't . . . I got really mad, you know, and I wrote this song in the heat of passion as it were . . . which is great for songwriting . . .

YOKO ONO: Or anger, shall we say?

JOHN LENNON: But getting a bit distant from it, it is expressing the losing you, of the eighteen months lost . . . it was everything . . . losing one's mother, losing one's everything – everything, losing everything you've ever lost is in that song.

88

That's losing whatever . . . but sparked by the fact that I couldn't get through on the damned phone. 'Can't even get you on the telephone.'

ANDY PEEBLES: And *Woman*, which I must say is a great favourite of mine.

JOHN LENNON: Oh thank you. I like that one, although I was sort of embarrassed because it . . . you know, sort of sounds a bit like *Girl* and a bit Beatley and a bit you know . . . but I do like it.

ANDY PEEBLES: Why does that embarrass you?

JOHN LENNON: Because I'm still a bit feeling that I'm supposed to be macho, Butch Cassidy or something and tough Lennon with the leather jacket, and swearing and all that . . . and I really am just as romantic as the next guy, you know, and I always was. It's the sort of eighties version of *Girl* to me, you know. I . . . like I refer to the other ones, Elvis, Orbison . . . I call this one the Beatle track all the time. I say, Oh, the Beatle track . . . let's do the Beatle track, and I . . . but to me it was . . . it suddenly dawned on me about the woman thing. I was in Bermuda again, and it suddenly sort of hit me about what women represent to us, not as the sex object or the mother, but just their contribution. That's why you hear me muttering at the beginning to the other half of the sky, which is Chairman Mao's famous statement. That it is the other half. You know all this thing about man, woman, man, woman, is a joke, you know. Without each other, there ain't nothing, you know. So it was like this sort of . . . my God, you know, it was a different viewpoint of what I'd felt about woman and I can't express it better than I said in the song. And it's for Yoko but it's to all women.

ANDY PEEBLES: John Peel, who we mentioned earlier . . .

JOHN LENNON: Ah, John . . . he's got no hair now . . . it was pretty thin then.

ANDY PEEBLES: He's losing it. I want to talk to you very briefly about what has been going on back home, while you've been here for five years.

JOHN LENNON: Yeah, I'd love to hear it.

ANDY PEEBLES: And ask you firstly for your views on the New Wave music that you must have heard, because you were telling me before we started recording and chatting, that there are a couple of stations in New York which have actually gone out on a limb and played some pretty fiery music, shall we say.

JOHN LENNON: Yeah, but they have started playing it . . . but that's only been with the last few months.

ANDY PEEBLES: Let me give you the quote from John Peel. He said to me before I left London: 'Tell John Lennon from me that I would be very interested to know if he had stayed in England, would he have championed the New Wave cause?''

JOHN LENNON: Yeah, I'm a champion of it now. I like it. You know, I mean, look when they catch up to the Yoko Ono Plastic Ono Band, then let him ask me that question again. They haven't reached that yet. Okay? So that's the answer to that. And anybody who thinks, Oh, well, dumb old Lennon just got stuck in the sixties to do *Starting Over* and *Losing You*, you think I don't know what she's doing? You think we went *Cold Turkey* and *Don't Worry Kyoko* and *Why* and *Open Your Box*. You can hear it all there. I'm aware of the B52's and Madness. 'Don't do that. Do this.' I think that is the most original thing actually because it's so peculiar. You know. I think out of all that mob that was one of the most original sounds. Very good drumming, very good bass and all that. Now, as I said, I was listening to the classical music and not really following it. I saw Sid Vicious die and all that on video in New York 'cos they were all coming over here to make it in the Big Apple as they call it. So, whoever came through, I could see them on this cable TV thing they have here. So I saw Blondie when she was unknown on the cable TV. I saw Vicious when he was living in the hotel being filmed and doing all that stuff, whenever that was, mid-seventies.

ANDY PEEBLES: How much of the Pistols music have you heard?

JOHN LENNON: Only whatever they did of video of it. You know there was a lot of videos of them down at Max's [New York night club], or wherever the hell they were, hanging out and playing . . . and Johnny Rotten and all that stuff. And yeah, great, to me initially on impact seeing all that, I thought, Oh that's how we used to behave at the Cavern before Brian told us to stop throwing up and sleeping on stage and swearing.

You know? I mean, like in Hamburg, I used to sleep on stage. We used to eat on stage. We used to swear on stage. We were absolutely *au naturel*. So . . . but nowadays they don't have to put a shine over on it to get a record contract, even though they are having a hard time with it. But still, yeah, I think it's great. I absolutely do. And when I was in Bermuda a guy that works for me, Fred Siemen had turned me onto the B52's, Lenny Loveritch or whatever her name is?

ANDY PEEBLES: Lene Lovich.

JOHN LENNON: Yeah, Madness . . . about two years ago, but then I wouldn't listen. I asked him to go out and make me some reggae records and put it on a cassette and on the other side he put all that stuff. B52's and all that . . . about two or three years ago, whenever they came out . . . and I wiped it out. I didn't even bother listening to it. I wasn't interested in anything other than what I was doing. But in Bermuda I said, Fred, what was all that stuff you give me? Go and get me it again. And he brought me Madness, B52's, Pretenders, and I said, Oh this is great. And he said, Well, I played . . . I gave it you two years ago. Why didn't you listen? I said, I didn't want to listen then. Now I want to hear what's going on. So I dig it.

ANDY PEEBLES: And you dig reggae too. Because you were saying that there are some stations here that actually play dub reggae.

JOHN LENNON: Oh they play dub . . . in the last ten years, the thing I missed most about England was reggae. And in the last ten years a lot of Caribbean people have come here from Haiti, from Jamaica and all points down there and they've created a whole community and the whole thing, and it's getting very hip, the reggae. Different from England's reggae. There's more R & B in it. Down in Brooklyn they're making it and it's very interesting – they play the English reggae and the New York reggae and the Island reggae – these are all different styles. And the dub reggae, they even, even the DJ's are on echo . . . on the echo, but listen to *Paper Shoes* – Yoko Ono's second album for the echo, for the dub. Okay? So for anybody who thinks we ain't hip, you know, when you catch up, then we can talk about it.

YOKO ONO: I mean we've done it all, really, you know.

JOHN LENNON: We've been there and back . . .

YOKO ONO: . . . and it started ten years ago, you know.

JOHN LENNON: . . . But I still like to do straight Rock 'n' Roll. *Losing You* is a straight blues. Forget about the lyrics. I could be singing *Ma Mammy done Gone*. It's blues – straight. *Starting Over* is straight pop rock, fifty style.

ANDY PEEBLES: What about the American music scene at the present moment? I found it a bit soft listening to the radio here. Particularly the rock stations.

JOHN LENNON: Well, each – they've gone top ten – FM was really – they played albums. The financial and all the things that get involved, things can never be always the same. So they're going through a change now, because they're WNEW and WPLJ – are the big white rock stations here, and they have started introducing a lot of – eh – what you call New Wave. But before they did it – a New Wave station opened, which just plays nothing but the clickety clickety click click, you know, whatever they call it, all the time, and it – of course, New York being what it is, they know what's going on in London 'cos people are coming back and going back and forth all the time so – it was in the air all the time. It was being played in clubs, it was talked about like underground, you know everything starts down there, and as soon as they make a hit record, whoever it is, everybody's going to say, They sold out! They sold out! And somebody else'll come with a blue nose and a green ass, you know, and that will be the new thing, so it has to move up and diffuse and become part of the scene. I did a TV show in 1973 with a guy called Tom Schneider, and he said, What music do you like? I said, Disco and reggae. I should have invested in reggae because I never thought the Americans would get on. The Beatles made an attempt at ska – the middle – the solo on *I Call Your Name* was ska – deliberate and conscious. Right.

ANDY PEEBLES: Mmmm. Yes.

JOHN LENNON: *Ob-la-di* was semi-semi. Okay? So, you know, you can't teach an old dog new tricks. Right? But I'm willing to learn anything. I dig it. I do enjoy it. I enjoy the best of it. I was in Bermuda in a disco. Okay, I finally went out one night to a disco. I haven't been to a disco since the Ad Lib [London night club of the sixties] days in London. Okay? And people were trying to get me to all these ones in New York. I just didn't want to know. They were saying, But it's different. It's different. I said, What? You mean more lights? You know. . . what the hell do I need to sit . . .

YOKO ONO: . . . or less lights.

JOHN LENNON: . . . sit there in the dark looking at all these weirdos . . . you know, I've got enough in me head. But I finally went with Fred, this guy that works with me, when we were separate – not separate for any reason – just a holiday. And I went there, and upstairs they were playing the disco, and downstairs, I walked in and they were playing *Rock Lobster* [a track by the B52's]. And I sort of said to him, Jesus, get the axe [rock slang for guitar] and call Mother [his affectionate name for Yoko]. She's finally made it. She mightn't be heard doing it, but they're doing her to a T. I mean they've studied her. They admit too. So I called her on the phone, and I said, You won't believe this, but I said, there's a group called B52's. I'd heard their name for years and years whenever they'd been around, but I'd never really listened. I said, There's somebody doing your act there. She won't listen to anything. You know, she absolutely is self-contained.

YOKO ONO: I said, Oh, I don't want to know, I don't want to know.

JOHN LENNON: I've sat her down and I said, Listen to it. I said, They're ready for you this time, kid. She said, Well, I'm not going to do the same old stuff again.

YOKO ONO: Because I did it ten years ago.

JOHN LENNON: I said, Do what you want, but do it. So here we are and we're doing it.

YOKO ONO: No, but you see, when Jack Douglas – I – he was assisting with all our albums that we made here, and he was very good, and when I called him, I, well of course, mmmm, when we decided to call him, I found out that in the five years that we were absent that he became a very famous producer – whatever, himself. All right. So we co-produce with him, and

93

so when he came, he said, Well, all these young people following you, you know. Sounds sort of silly, you know. So I said, No, no, really, really. All these people doing it. And I just still can't believe it. It's happening, I can see that. So but this time, Jack was saying, Well, you know, just show them, what old ways can do, you know that one. But I didn't intend to do it that way. That's why I understand what John means – John just did things that he wanted to do and what he would enjoy, you know, in this album.

JOHN LENNON: You see, we could have come back and tried to be freakier than the freaks.

YOKO ONO: We can do that.

JOHN LENNON: Make a conscious effort.

YOKO ONO: Because we were freakier ten years ago than these people.

JOHN LENNON: You know, we could have come back and just reissued the early stuff of Yoko's that really never got much air play. Oh maybe John Peel and you, and maybe a couple of people heard in London, a couple of people over here. But we didn't want to. We wanted to do the same as we did then, when we did whatever we were doing then.

ANDY PEEBLES: And you're obviously two very satisfied people on the strength of it.

JOHN LENNON: Yeah, we like doing it, that's the point, isn't it?

ANDY PEEBLES: One final question to you. What about your private life and your own sense of security these days? David Bowie has recently said that the great thing about New York is that he can walk down the street and people, instead of rushing up and ripping his clothes off, will come up, or rather will just walk past him and say, Hi, David, how are you? And he'd say, I'm very well. Is it the same for John and Yoko?

JOHN LENNON: Yeah, that's what made me finally stay here. It wasn't a conscious decision. I just found that I was going to movies, going to restaurants, and I had – the five years, you think, you know, it was just baking bread and the baby – no – because I went to Hong Kong and walked round. And people cannot appreciate what it was – when I left England I still couldn't go on the street. It was still Carnaby Street and all that stuff was going on. We couldn't walk around the block, couldn't go to a restaurant, unless you wanted to go 'with the business of the star going to the restaurant' garbage. I've even been walking the streets for the last seven years. When we first moved here, we actually lived in the village, in Greenwich Village, which is the sort of artsy-fartsy section of town, for those who don't know, where all the students and the would-bes live, you know? A few old poets and that. You know, people that have lived there for years, still live there. We got into this before – we didn't finish it – she told me that, Yes, you can walk on the street. You know. She says, You will be able to walk here; but I would be walking around tense like, waiting for somebody to say something, or jump on me, and it took me two years to unwind.I can go right out this door now and go in a restaurant. You want to know how great that is? Or go the movies? I mean, people come and ask for autographs or say, Hi, but they don't bug you, you know. They just – Oh, hey, how you doin'? Like your record. Because we've got a record out now, but before they'd shout, How you doing? You know. How's the baby? Oh, great thanks.

YOKO ONO: Talking about restaurants, I'm getting hungry.

JOHN LENNON: I'm starving too. What happened to the chicken soup?

ANDY PEEBLES: John, Yoko, on behalf of us, thank you very very much.

JOHN LENNON: A pleasure. It's a great pleasure to talk to you and the BBC and all the English, and Scots and Welsh and Irish listening.

ANDY PEEBLES: Cheers.

JOHN LENNON: Pip, pip, toot, toot.